SOVEREIGN

AND

UNBOUND

RECLAIM YOUR POWER.
ALIGN YOUR ENERGY.
LIVE ON YOUR OWN TERMS.

MEGAN A. JENIFER-HARRIS

TABLE OF CONTENTS

DEDICATION

Thank you Ted and Gwen.

Àwọn ará òrun.

Your life gave me wings.

May your Divine authority never fade.

Mo dúpẹ́, bàbá àti ìyá mi,

ara òrun, ìmúlòlùfé mi.

BEFORE WE BEGIN...

There are things we feel long before we can explain them. And sometimes, the deeper truths, the ones that move through the body like knowing, don't fit neatly into language.

Words will try but they won't always catch the full shape of what's being offered here.

So I ask you to read this book not just with your mind, but with your whole self — the part of you that listens for resonance, which recognizes truth, not because it's proven, but because it feels familiar...

...Remembered.

What's shared here may sound clear one moment and stir questions the next.

That's okay. Let it.

Some truths arrive gently. Others need time, space, or silence to unfold.

You may not agree with everything on these pages. And that's ok too. You're not meant to.

Take what feels right and savor it. Let the rest float. Parts may return to you later with new meaning, or not at all.

Both are fine.

Nonetheless, this book isn't asking you to believe anything. It's inviting you to feel... to remember... to reconnect...

To sense what's true for you.

So come as you are.

Bring your questions, your doubts, your softness, your brilliance.

There is room for all of it here.

Grace will meet you where you are.

And we'll begin from there.

WHAT HAPPENS WHEN
THE SCRIPT FAILS?

I used to think I was free. I followed the rules, did what I was told, and painted my life by numbers. I went to school, got the degrees, and graduated as valedictorian not once, but twice! Once in high school and again in my second master's degree program. I even graduated 6th in my undergraduate class from a prestigious university, one I was told would certainly set me up for a bright and stable future. I ticked all the boxes, did everything I was taught would lead to guaranteed success. I mean, I did everything right, didn't I?

So why did it still feel like something was missing?

Even as I pushed myself forward, there was always this nagging hum beneath the surface…

"Is this what I signed up for? Have I already put myself in a box? Am I ever going to be able to find sustainable work? Am I going to survive?"

I felt like I had been thrown into survival mode before I even started.

The Early Signs of Sovereignty

I had a wonderful childhood.

We were a singing family in the church. We all played instruments, and my mother would arrange songs for us. We traveled up and down the East Coast, singing and playing for the Lord.

Music wasn't just something we did; it was woven into our family's identity.

But even at age four, I felt disturbingly uncomfortable with singing.

I can still remember the feeling. It was like something inside me recoiled every time I had to do it. I never understood why. I just knew that, no matter how much I loved my family, singing never felt like mine.

… And yet, I did it anyway.

That discomfort stayed with me throughout my childhood. But when you're a child, you follow the rules. You trust that the grown-ups know best.

By the time I was a teenager, I started to get with the program. I sang like I was supposed to. I played my part.

But my first real act of sovereignty? That happened when I was six.

Our family had a system:

First child: clarinet.

Second child: flute.

Third child: clarinet.

Fourth child: flute.

It was my turn. As the fourth child, I was supposed to play the flute. That was the pattern. That was what had been decided for me.

But something inside me knew better.

"No, Daddy! I want to play the violin!"

I still remember the words leaving my mouth… the boldness… the defiance.

I was six when I declared it, and seven when I got to start.

That was my little soul beginning to express sovereignty.

It wouldn't be the last time.

There were other moments, other instances throughout my childhood where I sensed that something wasn't quite aligning. But I was still growing up. And when you're growing up, the rules and the scripts come from the grown-ups.

So, I followed the script even when something inside me was already starting to question it.

The Moment Everything Changed

All of that questioning… the quiet awareness that something didn't quite fit… was nothing compared to what was coming next.

When I was 22, barely scratching the surface of adulthood, my father passed away.

Suddenly. Unexpectedly.

My birthday was only a couple of months before, and I wasn't even home when he transitioned. I was in another state, finishing up an internship, thinking about my second senior year of college, completely unaware that in just a few moments, my life was about to split into a *before* and an *after*.

My mother called…

There was a pause. Just the faintest hesitation before she spoke. Like she was gathering the strength to say the words.

Her voice wasn't choked up, but I heard the weight of it. The way she had to push it out.

At first, she faintly said, "He died." I blinked. "Huh? What did you say?" Then, more clearly, she repeated herself. "Megan, your father died." No buildup. No way to soften the blow. Just a sentence that changed my world.

Reaching for Stability

I was running on fumes.

I had made it through that final senior year on autopilot, but my grief had no outlet. I never stopped to process it. I just kept moving, kept achieving, kept pretending that if I could keep all the pieces together, then maybe I wouldn't fall apart.

But inside, I was lost. Untethered. A zombie on autopilot.

And then, there was him...

A guy... A student at my school. Just like me.

Unlike me, his plan seemed solid. More certain. More guaranteed. I had a plan too! But after my father's death, my path felt unstable, like the ground beneath me had shifted. His, on the other hand, looked like a straight line. He was already on a defined track toward law school. Structured, stable, predictable. And maybe most importantly, he had met my father just a month before he passed. That felt significant, so I clung to him. Not because I was weak, but because I was tired of feeling like I was floating with no direction.

At first, it made sense. But certainty and alignment are *not* the same thing.

I told myself it would work. That he was my stability and guide forward. So, when he proposed, I said "yes." I moved hundreds of miles away and got a temp job in finance. I started to build a life around him. For almost a year, I convinced myself that this was it. I told myself that I had found the thing, the person, that would finally anchor me.

But deep down, something wasn't sitting right.

As I became stronger in my own thinking, we began to clash. The tension built, the differences became undeniable, and eventually, we separated. I left, came back home, and re-enrolled to finish my MBA. In hindsight, I credit him, *my angel*, for helping me grow into a shifting perspective. Being in relationship with him was pivotal to my sovereignty and unbinding, even though we didn't stay together. He wasn't my forever person, but he was the person who helped me start to see.

To this day, I believe our paths crossing was Divine alignment. His role wasn't to stay. His role was to open the door. And once you start seeing the cracks, you can't unsee them.

The Realization: Sovereignty Begins Here

I wrote this book to help you see the scripts, the conditioning, the invisible threads shaping your path, and to help you begin unbinding yourself from them.

Sovereign & Unbound is structured in three parts, each guiding you through the process of reclaiming your power:

Part I: Foundations of the Soul and Divine Blueprint

Part II: The Unbinding Process (through the three gates: Illusions, Release, and Embodiment)

Part III: Living Unbound

Each chapter will take you deeper, unraveling the layers that have kept you bound to a script you didn't consciously choose.

You've carried the weight of everything.

Now, it's time to feel what it's like to be held.

Turn the page, and let's begin.

PART I

FOUNDATIONS OF THE SOUL AND DIVINE BLUEPRINT

"You are not a drop in the ocean. You are the entire ocean in a drop."

- Rumi

Before we can reclaim our sovereignty, we must FIRST understand who we TRULY are. Beyond the roles, the conditioning, and the expectations placed upon us, there is something ancient. There is something enduring.

That "something" is *The Soul*.

But what IS the soul? And how do we know we even have one? This section begins with the book's foundation: the *nature* of the soul, our cosmic origins, and the unseen forces shaping our existence.

CHAPTER 1

THE NATURE OF THE SOUL

The first time I became aware of myself, like *truly* aware, I was no older than eight or nine. We traveled a lot by camper and motorhome. I remember a very specific time, where I was tucked into the wide seat of our motorhome as it rumbled down an endless stretch of highway.

My dad was at the helm of this beastly machine, one steady hand on the wheel, his gaze locked on the road ahead as if he and the motorhome were in silent agreement about where we were going. My mom sat beside him, his quiet and calm passenger, her presence like a soft anchor in the ever-moving world. She rarely said much while we traveled, but I could feel her: a kind of peaceful watchfulness, as if she were listening to something beyond what the rest of us could hear.

Behind them, my brothers were scattered across the cabin, lost in their own worlds. At least one sprawled at the dinette table, pencil in hand, working on drawing a comic book. Another actually flipping through the pages of a real comic book, occasionally muttering under his breath when he got excited by a particular part. The third one, closest to age with me, was between falling asleep and trying to refrain from saying that he was bored. Being bored was considered a "bad word" in our family.

Then there was me.

I didn't have a book or a puzzle. No pencil, no paper. Just a window, a seat, and a vast world rolling by. At first, I was just watching... the trees bending in the wind... the telephone poles ticking by like steady markers of time… the sky stretching out endlessly above it all. The road curved and straightened, curved and straightened, but inside the motorhome, everything felt steady. Safe. Familiar.

And then, *something shifted.*

It was subtle, like a change in air pressure or the moment between inhaling and exhaling.

I was still watching, still aware of the world outside. But suddenly I realized something else.

I am here.

Not just as a body, not just as a little girl in a moving home on wheels, but as something separate from it all. A presence behind my own eyes. I could feel myself watching. Not just the trees or the road or the sky, but *me*. The *"me"* that noticed, that wondered, that existed beyond the motion of my hands… the sound of my own breathing… my body weight pressed into the seat.

The motorhome moved forward, but the part of me that noticed, *wasn't moving at all*. It was just *there*. Still.

I blinked, testing the feeling, shifting slightly in my seat as if to make sure I was still in my body. My fingers curled and uncurled in my lap. I turned my head, taking in my family, each lost in their own world. Everything was as it had been moments ago, yet something in me had changed.

Who is the *"me"* that sees?

It wasn't a question I had ever been taught to ask. It wasn't something I could have put into words at the time. But I felt it in my bones, in the quiet spaces of my being. I was not just in the world. I was experiencing it. And somehow, that made me separate from it, apart from the totality of everything moving around me.

The thought lingered… delicate and vast, like a whisper in a great, open room.

And then, as easily as it came, it disappeared. My brothers laughed at something ridiculous. My dad turned the wheel ever so slightly, the hum of the road unchanged beneath us. The motorhome kept moving, and I let myself slip back into its rhythm… into the warmth of the familiar… into the simple act of being.

But the knowledge never left me.

I carried it with me from that day forward, tucked into the quiet places of my mind, waiting for the moment I would understand.

Defining the Soul through Perspectives Across Time

At some point, we all have a moment like this: An instant where we recognize the presence of ourselves. Maybe it happens in childhood, or maybe later, in the pause between thoughts or in the silence between words. But at some point, we notice: I am not just my body. I am not just my thoughts. I am here, witnessing it all! Every culture and every wisdom tradition has tried to define what THAT is… what we *truly* are beneath the surface.

The soul is the essence of who you are: your unique energetic imprint, the part of you that carries your experiences, your lessons and your individuality across time. It holds your memories, your emotions, and the deep inner wisdom that transcends a single lifetime. The soul is personal and shaped by its journey, yet always connected to something greater.

Spirit, on the other hand, is different. **Spirit is the animating force**, the Divine Breath that gives life to all things. It is universal and *untouched by identity*. It is formless energy flowing through everything. If the soul is the *thread* of your existence, then spirit is the *vast ocean* in which that thread is woven.

We will explore Spirit more deeply in Chapter 4, but for now, we will focus on the soul: *the part of you that remains uniquely you across lifetimes, experiences and every version of your becoming.*

Throughout history, different cultures have described the soul in ways that reflect its continuity and individuality:

- **Ancient Egyptians** believed in the ba, the unique personality of the soul that could move between the living and the afterlife. The ka was its life force, but the ba was what made a person distinct, carrying their essence beyond physical existence.

- **In Hinduism**, the soul (atman) is considered eternal, moving through cycles of reincarnation. While Brahman represents the ultimate Divine reality (*akin to spirit*), the *atman* is the individual essence, learning and evolving through lifetimes.

- Many **Indigenous traditions** see the soul as deeply tied to ancestral memory. It is not just a personal essence but a continuation of lineage, carrying the wisdom of those who came before.

- **Greek philosophy** described the soul (psyche) as the true self, distinct from the body, moving toward wisdom and higher understanding over time.

These perspectives all point to a universal truth: the soul is what makes you *You*, across time and space. It carries the imprint of your existence, and evolves with each experience, yet it also always holds the core of your being.

But what if we go deeper? What if we strip away the religious and cultural interpretations and look at it through a different lens?

Stardust Incarnate

Science tells us that every atom in our body was forged in the heart of a dying star. The iron in our blood, the calcium in our bones, the oxygen in our lungs... all of it contains remnants of carbon and cosmic explosions that happened billions of years ago.

We are not separate from the universe; *we are the universe*, embodied.

Although I tend to write poetically, this perspective is the discovery of physics, chemistry, and biology–the very tangible structure of existence! If we accept that we are composed of ancient elements, why would our essence, **our soul**, be any different? Why wouldn't we carry echoes of something beyond just this single lifetime?

The Timeless Essence of the Soul

Most of what shapes us comes from this lifetime. It shows up as the conditioning of our families, the beliefs passed down through generations and experiences we absorb like secondhand smoke. But sometimes, there are things that can't be explained by memory alone.

An example of this would be the child who speaks a language they've never learned. Another example could be deep, unshakable fears that seem to have no root in personal experience, or even the uncanny recognition or feeling of "home" of a place you've never been. Some call these past life echoes. Others see them as ancestral imprints, which are energies passed down through bloodlines, like genetic memory but on a spiritual level.

Not everyone resonates with the idea of past lives, and that's okay. What matters is recognizing that we are shaped by more than just the immediate and the obvious. Some influences stretch beyond what we can see, yet they leave fingerprints on our being all the same.

A Final Thought: The Soul as a Compass

What does this mean for sovereignty? Why does understanding the soul matter?

Because the first step in reclaiming your power is remembering that you were never just this name, this job, this history. You are something much older… much freer. The illusion is that you were *ever* just this moment in time.

We are, *and always have been,* unbound.

Chapter 1 Recap:

So far, we have explored the truth that you are more than your body, your history, or the identity you've been given. Beneath the surface of your experiences, there is something unshakable: an awareness that has always existed, untouched by time or circumstance.

Every culture and every wisdom tradition point to this knowing:

The soul is eternal, deeply connected, and inherently whole.

And yet, despite this wholeness, many of us move through life feeling disconnected from it. Somewhere along the way, the clarity of our inner knowing… *the intuitive sense of who we truly are…* becomes clouded. Not because it disappears, but because we are conditioned to look everywhere *except* within.

In Chapter 2 we turn toward that lost clarity.

Before the world told you who to be, before you were shaped by expectations and external definitions, you carried something unaltered: *Your Divine Blueprint.* This is not something you must earn or prove worthy of; it has been with you from the beginning.

But what happens when we stop listening? What happens when we are taught, explicitly or subtly, that we are incomplete and that we must strive, perform, or conform to be whole?

Before we can reclaim what has always been ours, we must recognize the ways we've been led to forget it

CHAPTER 2

RECLAIMING YOUR

DIVINE BLUEPRINT

Think about blueprints for a house. The design is set before anything is built. The walls, the foundation, the layout... it's all mapped out in advance. Now, once construction starts, adjustments might happen. Materials might change, workers might come and go, weather conditions might delay things. But the original blueprint? It remains the reference point.

Your *Divine Blueprint* works similarly.

It is the core structure of who you are. It is the energetic framework you were born with. It maps the way your energy is built to flow, the rhythm that feels natural to you and the patterns that keep showing up in your life no matter how much you try to override them. While life, healing, and external influences may change how it gets expressed, the core design does not change.

What is the Divine Blueprint?

Your Divine Blueprint is the *unshakable foundation of You*. It's the natural tendencies, strengths, and energetic patterns that shape how you move through the world. Its why certain things come naturally to you, while others always feel like an uphill battle. Its why certain environments energize you, while others leave you drained. It's why some paths feel aligned, while others feel forced... no matter how much effort you put in. Some call this destiny, soul contracts, or cosmic agreements, but you don't need to subscribe to any of those terms to recognize this truth:

There is a version of you that feels the *most* real. The *most* natural. The *most* right.

And that version has been with you *all along*.

The Ugly Duckling Was Never Ugly

There's a story you've likely heard before: the tale of The Ugly Duckling. A bird is born among ducks, but from the start, it doesn't fit in. Its body is shaped differently, its movements aren't the same, and no matter how hard it tries, it just doesn't belong. So, it internalizes the belief that something is wrong. It spends its life trying to keep up with the ducks, wondering why it always feels so out of place. It shrinks itself, hoping to blend in. It questions whether it's broken, defective, or simply not good enough.

But then one day, it sees a group of swans and something stirs inside it… a deep recognition. When it looks at its own reflection in the water, it finally sees the truth:

It was never a duck. It was a swan all along.

The "ugliness" wasn't real. The problem was never the bird itself. It was the environment, the expectations, and the false belief that it needed to conform to something it was never designed to be.

This is what happens when you try to live outside your Divine Blueprint. You struggle not because you're broken, but because you're trying to fit into something that was never meant for you. You were never meant to move like a duck. You were built to soar like a swan.

And the moment you *recognize* that truth, everything changes. And I mean EVERYTHING.

Life Will Try to Override It

The problem? The world doesn't always encourage you to live in alignment with your natural design. Instead, it hands you scripts telling you who you should be, what you should prioritize, and how you should operate.

- If you're naturally introspective, you might have been told to be more "outgoing."

- If you move through life at a steady, deliberate pace, you may have been pressured to "hurry up."

- If you're wired to flow with spontaneity, you may have been conditioned to over-plan and over-structure.

Over time, you start editing yourself to fit external expectations, suppressing the parts of you that don't align with what's "acceptable" or "successful." But here's the thing:

No matter how much you try to override your natural wiring, your Divine Blueprint remains.

You may bury it. You may ignore it. You may try to force yourself into a different mold. But the core structure of who you are will always be there, waiting for you to return to it.

The Role of Healing & Change

Now, let's be clear. Life is dynamic. Your experiences, choices, and environment can influence how you *express* your blueprint.

Think of it like this:

- Healing work doesn't change the blueprint. It removes the debris covering it.

- Life circumstances don't erase your design. They affect how freely it can be expressed.

- Planetary shifts, seasons of life, and external influences don't rewrite the blueprint. They impact how it unfolds.

Just like celestial movements can change how you feel or respond to life, external factors can influence your expression. But at your core, your original wiring, the way you are built to operate, remains intact. This means that personal growth isn't always about becoming a "better" version of yourself. It's more so about *aligning more deeply* with what was *always* true.

But What If...? (Because I'm pretty sure some doubts have crept up...)

Some may ask, *"Isn't it enough to rely on my intellect and proven methods?"* Your intellect is valuable. Your strategies, logic, and learned experiences all play an important role. But your Divine Blueprint isn't something you figure out. It's something you recognize. There is a difference between learning about yourself and *remembering* yourself. When you work against your Divine Blueprint, everything feels like a battle. You push, struggle, and force yourself into ways of being that don't fit. When you work *with* it, things flow. Not because life is suddenly easy, but because you are moving in harmony with how you were designed to operate.

And then there's another common fear:

"I've been told I need to fix myself."

Healing isn't necessarily about fixing yourself. Alignment isn't about changing yourself. It's about *removing* what is *in the way* of your **natural state**. You were *never* broken to begin with. The real work isn't about becoming something new. Instead, it's about unlearning what *took you away* from yourself.

The Invitation: Come Back to Yourself

Reclaiming your Divine Blueprint is an act of trust...

Trust that you were designed a certain way for a reason.

Trust that you don't need to force yourself into something unnatural.

Trust that alignment feels like ease... not because life is always easy, but because you're no longer fighting yourself.

The world has spent years convincing you to doubt your own design. But what if the thing you've been searching for has been with you all along? What if peace, clarity, and confidence aren't things you achieve, but instead, things you *return* to?

This is the invitation...

To come *home* to yourself. To recognize what was never lost. To move through life not as someone trying to *"figure it all out,"* but as someone who *already knows* and is simply **remembering**.

... Because you were never meant to be a duck.

You were born to be a swan.

And now, it's time to own that truth.

Chapter 2 Recap:

Your Divine Blueprint has always been there... steady, intact, and waiting. The work isn't about becoming someone new; it's about trusting who you've always been.

But if alignment is natural, why do so many of us *struggle* to live it?

Before you can move freely in your blueprint, you must FIRST see what has been *shaping* you without your conscious consent.

In Chapter 3, we begin The Unbinding Process, starting with the *unseen forces* that have influenced your reality from the beginning. This is step one in the reclamation of your naturally unbound state–to recognize what has been subtly and quietly keeping you from your sovereignty.

CHAPTER 3

UNSPOKEN LIMITS AND
HIDDEN INFLUENCES

When I was a kid, I asked "why" A LOT! Not to be difficult. I just wanted to understand things. If a rule existed, I figured there *had* to be a reason. But when I asked my dad why we did certain things a certain way, his answer was always the same:

"Because I said so."

End of discussion. No explanation, no conversation. Just a full stop.

For a long time, I accepted that. I didn't realize how much it shaped me. Not just in that moment, but in the years that followed. I learned that some things weren't meant to be questioned. I learned that authority had the final word. Even if something didn't make sense, my job was to *follow* the rule, not to *understand* it. I did what I was told and unfortunately, shrank in the process.

I had NO CLUE that I had never learned to think critically. Not until after my dad passed. Because that's when I really had to start figuring things out for myself. And once I started questioning one thing, the floodgates opened!

Why had I spent years making decisions based on rules I never chose?

Why had I been living within invisible boundaries that no one had even told me existed?

Why had I accepted so much without asking whether it truly aligned with me?

That's when I realized: **some of the biggest limits in my life were the ones I never thought to question.**

The Limits You Can't See Are Oftentimes the Ones That Hold You Back

We all inherit unspoken rules. Not just from family, but from culture, religion, education, and the environments we move through every day.

Some are clear and direct:

- *"You need a degree to be successful."*

- *"You have to work twice as hard to be respected."*

- *"People like us don't do things like that."*

But others are so ingrained they don't even feel like rules. They just feel like the truth.

- Maybe you were always the responsible one, so you automatically take on more than your share, even when it's unfair.

- Maybe you were raised in a home where emotions weren't talked about, so now you struggle to express yourself, even with people you trust.

- Maybe you learned that questioning authority was "disrespectful," so even now, as an adult, you hesitate to challenge what doesn't sit right with you.

These aren't just personal habits. They are *programming*, and programming doesn't just magically disappear when you grow up. Programming runs in the background, subtly and consistently shaping your decisions without you even realizing it.

Success Doesn't Necessarily Mean You're Free

A lot of people assume that if they've achieved success, they've broken free from their limits. But that's not always true.

Ask yourself: *"Did I choose this life, or did it choose me?"*

- If you're wildly successful but constantly exhausted, was the path really yours? Or were you taught that your worth is measured by how much you produce?

- If you always put others first but feel drained, was that a conscious choice? Or did you inherit the belief that your value comes from self-sacrifice?

- If you have financial security but still feel unfulfilled, was this truly your dream? Or did you follow a blueprint someone else handed you?

Even freedom, when defined by someone else's standards, can be a form of limitation.

The Cost of Never Asking "Why"

Many people resist this idea.

"I don't feel controlled. I make my own decisions."

But conditioning isn't about feeling controlled. It's about the choices you never even realized were possible! For some, the impact of this is subtle, like limiting their career choices, influencing their relationships, or impacting their ability to express themselves fully. But for others, the conditioning runs so deep that they truly believe there is no alternative.

Cult survivors often speak about this in ways that are chillingly familiar. Many didn't realize they had a choice because they were taught there was no world outside of what they were given. Their entire reality was constructed around the idea that questioning was dangerous, that leaving was impossible and that anything outside of their belief system was a lie. And even after leaving, the conditioning lingers. It takes a while to unlearn the idea that freedom was *always* an option.

The same pattern plays out in more subtle ways in everyday life. No, not everyone is raised in a cult, but many ARE raised inside mental frameworks that make alternatives feel impossible. Family systems, rigid traditions, high-control religious environments, oppressive cultural norms: ALL of these can function in ways that keep people from *ever* realizing there was a question to ask in the first place!

Think about the last major decision you made. Why did you make it?

Was it based on a deep inner knowing?

Or was it influenced by expectation, fear, or "the way things have always been done?"

Some limits are so deeply embedded that they feel real. But just because you don't see a boundary doesn't mean it isn't there.

Where Your Power Begins

For YEARS, I didn't think to challenge the things I had been taught. But when my dad was gone, and I no longer had him telling me what to do, I had to start figuring things out for myself. My mom was still alive, but I didn't look to her in the same way. She was present, loving, supportive... but she wasn't the one who had shaped my sense of authority. My dad was the one who set the rules, the one who had the final say, the one whose voice I had internalized as the ultimate authority. And when he was gone, that voice wasn't there to answer my questions.

At first, I thought I just needed to find new answers. But what I really needed was to start asking different questions... And that's when I realized something:

The greatest gift my dad ever gave me wasn't the rules. It was the moment I had to *break free* from them.

Not in a way that dishonored him. Not in a way that dismissed everything he taught me, but in a way that let me take what served me and leave the rest behind.

I'm not suggesting to throw away everything you've been taught. Instead, this chapter is really about *finally choosing* what belongs to you

Chapter 3 Recap:

You're still here! That means you're invested in your liberation! Here is what we have uncovered so far:

- Some of the biggest limits in your life are the ones you never thought to question.

- Just because you're successful doesn't mean you're free. Success can be shaped by hidden conditioning.

- Real freedom starts when you stop accepting *"because that's just how it is"* and start asking, *"Do I actually believe this?"*

What's Next: Stepping Beyond the Invisible Walls

Everything we've explored so far has been about recognition… seeing the illusions, the weight you've carried, and the limits you never questioned. But awareness alone isn't enough. You can know a cage exists and still sit inside it.

This is where everything shifts.

As we move into Part II, the focus changes from *seeing* the bindings to *breaking them*. This is where the real work begins.

In the next chapter, we'll talk about what happens when you start rewriting the rules. What happens when you push past the edges of what you've been told is possible.

Because once you step beyond the invisible walls, there's no going back.

THE UNBINDING PROCESS

"When I dare to be powerful - to use my strength in the service of my vision - then it becomes less and less important whether I am afraid."

- Audre Lorde

You've started to see the invisible forces that have shaped you... the beliefs, expectations, and limits you never thought to question. But seeing them is just the beginning.

Now comes the real work.

Unbinding is not about gaining power. Unbinding is about *reclaiming what has always been yours!* It's about realizing that freedom isn't just the *absence* of limitation; it's the *presence* of choice! It's the realization that true sovereignty doesn't come from anything outside of you. It comes from within.

In this next section, we'll explore what happens when you start rewriting the rules. We'll confront the discomfort of stepping outside familiar frameworks, the resistance that comes with choosing your own path, and the responsibility that comes with real freedom.

This is where unbinding becomes action... where expansion becomes possible!

Where you stop asking for permission and *start trusting what has been yours all along!*

Let's begin.

THE GATE OF ILLUSIONS

Initiation: Shining a Light on the Unseen

As you're probably well aware by now, I was always a curious child. My mind was constantly reaching, stretching beyond what was handed to me as truth, but I learned early that some questions weren't welcomed… (especially in church.)

Like many of us were, I was raised in church, but my experience wasn't limited to one congregation. My family worshiped at one primary church, but because we were often guest musicians at other churches, I witnessed a wide range of worship styles. Some churches were quiet and reverent. Others were loud and filled with shouting and praise breaks. Some leaned heavily on doctrine, while others focused on personal revelation.

But no matter where we went, one thing remained consistent. There were *rules* about how you were *allowed* to engage with God.

One Sunday, I asked my mom something simple but dangerous:

"If God already knows everything, why do we have to tell Him what we did wrong? Shouldn't He already know?"

Again, I wasn't trying to be difficult. I *genuinely* wanted to understand. But the look I got from her told me I had stepped over some invisible line. Instead of a thoughtful response, I was met with something much sharper: *"Because that's what the Bible says. That's what we're supposed to do."*

That was it. No explanation. No discussion. Just a rule. *Because I said so.*

Something in me shrank at that moment. Not because I believed I had asked the wrong question, but because I realized asking questions wasn't safe. I learned to keep my thoughts to myself. And yet, even as I sat quietly, I felt things I couldn't unfeel. I noticed things I wasn't supposed to notice. Like the fact that some people who preached forgiveness the loudest were often the least forgiving. Or that the same adults who taught us that God loved us unconditionally seemed to believe He would throw us away the moment we "fell short," or even worse, act like He didn't know us if he felt jaded by our relationship.

Even as a child, I could sense the contradiction. But… because I had been taught to trust external authority more than my own discernment, I silenced my knowing.

The Lie of Separation from God & The Illusion of Guilt

All of that was my first encounter with **The Gate of Illusions…** the moment when something felt off, but I overrode my own wisdom to stay on board with what I was being taught.

What is the greatest illusion of all?

The belief that we are separate from God.

This illusion is the *foundation* of control. If people believe they are inherently disconnected from Source, they become easy to manipulate. If they believe they must earn Divine approval, they will stay locked in guilt-driven cycles of obedience, always striving but never arriving.

Guilt is one of the *strongest* emotional weapons used to keep people bound to illusion. In religious spaces, it's often framed as "conviction," a sign that God is displeased, that you've done something wrong, and that you must repent to regain Divine favor. But guilt is not a Divine directive. It is an *energetic response* to something not adding up in the life you desire to live and the life you're actually living.

We have been conditioned to believe that guilt is a sign of *God's displeasure*, such that when we feel guilt, it must mean we have stepped out of Divine favor, requiring penance, sacrifice, or spiritual "correction." But guilt, when understood correctly, is not about punishment. Energetically, guilt is about dissonance and ultimately resonance.

The emotion of guilt is what happens when your internal frequency no longer matches what you once believed to be true. If you believe in a separate, emotionally reactive God, guilt becomes a moral burden. Guilt acts like "proof" that you are inherently flawed and need fixing. But if you understand that you and God are not separate, guilt is no longer about "sin" or Divine disapproval. Instead, it is a *misalignment between your current self and your evolving awareness.*

Many spiritual traditions assign human qualities to God, making God out to be a judge, a parent, an overseer with opinions and emotions. But God is not human. God is not reactive. God does not have fleeting emotions or keep a report card of your wrongs. These are *human narratives* placed on Divinity to make it more relatable, but in doing so, they distort the truth.

God is genderless. God is formless. God is even opinionless.

If God is truly omnipresent, then God is *within* you, *not* separate from you. And if that is indeed true, then your desires, your deepest callings and your most profound knowing, are not just yours. They are Divine!

So, when guilt arises, don't rush to self-condemnation. Instead, pause and ask:

Is this guilt a sign that I am a bad person?

Or is this guilt showing me where I am out of alignment with my truth?

When you remove the illusion of separation, you stop seeing guilt as a moral failure and start recognizing it for what it is, which is an *invitation back into alignment.*

Religious institutions have long reinforced the concept of separation and guilt by anthropomorphizing God... giving the Infinite Field of Consciousness human-like emotions of anger, jealousy, and conditional love. We've been conditioned to believe in a God who withholds, who doles out approval and punishment based on performance, much like an earthly parent.

But if God is not an emotionally reactive being, if God is not a cosmic parent grading us on our behavior, then what happens to the concepts of guilt, shame, and piety?

They collapse.

What remains is pure alignment. Not striving, not suffering. Just resonance.

This concept is not new. Many spiritual traditions have taught this truth for thousands of years:

- **In Ancient Kemet** (*Egyptian mysticism*), God (NTR) was not a separate being, but an all-pervasive force moving through all things. The idea of Divine separation was a distortion. The real work was about restoring balance with Ma'at.

- **In Hindu philosophy** (*Advaita Vedanta*), the greatest illusion (Maya) is the belief that we are anything other than Divine.

- **In Christianity**, Jesus himself said, "You are gods." (John 10:34 NIV). When Jesus said this, He was referencing Psalm 82:6, which says, "I said, 'You are gods; you are all children of the Most High.'" This was not blasphemy. It was a reminder. Jesus wasn't saying that humans should try to *become* Divine. He was revealing that they *already were!* Jesus was a mirror incarnate, reflecting back to humanity our innate Divinity.

- **In Ifá**, Divinity is accessed through Orí, the Higher Self. While Babalawos (Baba) and Ìyánífá (Ìyá) serve as intermediaries in formal divination, Orí is not dependent on them. It is always present and always guiding.

Each of these traditions points to the same truth: *we were never separate to begin with.* Religion has long distorted this truth, convincing people that they are powerless, separate, and in need of an external source to connect them to God. I get it and empathize. People generally need structure, so spiritual traditions have created frameworks... rules and steps to follow.

Energy, Witchcraft, and the Frameworks We Fear

One of the greatest fears people have been taught is the fear of their own power.

This is most evident in how we talk about witchcraft. The word alone carries weight. It conjures images of darkness, deception and evil. But what most people call witchcraft is often nothing more than misunderstood energy work, ancestral wisdom, and natural law in motion.

People rebuke "witchcraft" while simultaneously anointing others with oil, laying on hands, or taking communion. These are all rituals. These are all forms of energy movement. The difference is the framework.

Witchcraft, in its truest sense, is about intention. It's about aligning with elemental forces, working with unseen energy, directing willpower, and honoring natural cycles. It is not evil. It is not demonic. But centuries of colonization, patriarchy, and religious control have labeled it as such to keep people from their own intuitive power.

In many African spiritual systems, what outsiders call "witchcraft" is simply reverence. It is the honoring of ancestors. The making of offerings. The intuitive knowing that what is seen is never the whole story. In Ifá, for instance, divination is not about predicting doom. It's about understanding energetic patterns so you can realign with harmony. Working with Òrìṣà is not idol worship. Many commonly confuse this with worshiping the creator's creations. This simply isn't the case. It's about honoring aspects of nature and consciousness that *already* live within you.

The truth is: **energy doesn't care about labels.** You can call it witchcraft, prayer, spellwork, or a prophetic word. What matters is *the frequency*, *the force*, and *the intention* behind it.

This is why different people can operate within *completely different* traditions and *still* be blessed! Someone can speak in tongues, dance in the Spirit, and be met by the Divine. Another can sing Òrìṣà songs, light candles, and make offerings, *and also* be met by the Divine. Because energy moves where alignment flows.

Religious frameworks are just that—frameworks. They are not the source. They are not the power itself. They are not the *only* way.

This ties directly into another primary illusion…

The Illusion of a "Right" Framework

An extremely potent illusion in spirituality is the belief that there is only ONE *correct* way to access the Divine. Religious traditions, spiritual practices, and cultural customs function as energy-moving frameworks. They provide structure, but they are not the source of power itself.

- A tongue-speaking, oil-slinging, Holy Ghost-filled, prophesying Christian can be deeply aligned within their framework.

- A devoted Òrìṣà practitioner, making offerings and honoring their lineage, can be equally aligned in their practice.

- The power isn't in the framework itself. The power is in the *alignment* and energy movement *within* it.

People are drawn to rules and structures because they give them a sense of direction, but no single system is the *ultimate* truth.

This is where *The Gate of Illusions* traps people. If they believe their way is the *only* way, they become blind to the fact that MANY frameworks move energy effectively. The structure may look different, but the results, *when done in true alignment*, are the same.

The Illusion of Separation Between Science & Spirituality

Here's another illusion that distorts our perception. It's the false separation between science and spirituality. Many assume that frequency and vibration are just metaphors... that when spiritual traditions speak of "high vibrational states" or "resonance," they are using poetic language rather than describing a tangible, measurable reality.

But this *too*, is an illusion.

Science is finally catching up to what ancient wisdom has always known. Dr. Valerie Hunt's research on electromagnetic fields, cymatics experiments demonstrating sound's precise geometric influence on matter, and modern studies by Joe Dispenza, Caroline Cory, and Lisa Alexander[1] all confirm that frequency is a structured, mathematical force, not just mystical abstraction.

Yet, despite this growing body of evidence, many spiritualists reject science and many scientists dismiss energy work... both clinging to an outdated divide that was never real to begin with. The truth is, resonance is real, and frequency is not subjective. Frequency is fundamental to our lived experience.

A Light Introduction to the Afterlife Illusion

For many, life is not about living.

It's about preparing to die.

---

[1] Appendix B & C: Science, Spirituality & Energy Intelligence / References

** pause **

Think about that…

The fear of the afterlife (*or settlement on a belief in a better life beyond this dimension*) has shaped how people behave, coercing them into rigid obedience rather than conscious alignment. Some spend their lives *avoiding sin* instead of *seeking truth*. They silence their desires, suppress their curiosity, and limit their joy… all because of a belief that this life is just a test, a temporary struggle to prove worthiness for the next.

But what if that's another illusion?

What if the point was never about proving yourself for the afterlife, but *fully embodying Divinity right here, right now?*

What if the afterlife is not a place you earn but simply a continuation of how you've chosen to live?

Intuitive Perception: Cutting Through Illusion

I learned early that energy speaks louder than words. When I was a college freshman, I attended the same university as my three older brothers. One day, an upperclassman stopped me outside a dorm and said something that made me pause:

"The devil is going to try to use you because you're the black sheep of your family."

I didn't know this dude for real. He knew my brothers, but he didn't know me. And yet, he felt entitled to speak something over my life as if he had Divine authority. For a moment, it rattled me. But I trusted my knowing, and my knowing said *this ain't right.*

I reached out to one of my brothers, the one who knew the Bible like the back of his hand. He listened, gave me scriptures, and asked me questions that made me reflect, but he did not condemn me.

The real lesson came later.

I realized that I didn't require any overt sign of danger to know something was off. My body felt it. My spirit knew it. I didn't need proof. I needed to trust my *knowledge*. So, I did. I stayed away from him. I paid attention. I became more aware of when people used religion as a tool to exert control over others.

Conditioning teaches people, especially women, to ignore their instincts. Conditioning causes people to override their discomfort, or doubt what they feel, and to relinquish trust in external authority instead. Nonetheless, that day, I *listened* to my intuition.

The Egregore Effect: When Belief Becomes an Entity

Some illusions are not just personal. They're collective! They gain power through agreement, through repetition and through ritual. Over time, they become actual self-sustaining forces.

These are known as **egregores**: energetic entities born from collective thought, emotion, and belief. Yup! An entity.

Egregores feed off of attention and fear. They thrive on repetition and consensus. And one of the most dangerous modern egregores in the spiritual and political landscape is **Christian Nationalism**.

Christian Nationalism didn't just pop up out of nowhere. It has roots in the early 1900s, woven into white supremacist ideology and wrapped in scripture to justify hierarchy, exclusion, and control. It operates like an energetic parasite—hijacking sincere faith and twisting it into a tool of domination. Under the guise of "protecting the nation," it binds spirituality to power structures that reinforce separation and supremacy.

This is about consciousness (not religion)! Egregores, like this one, warp the frequency of collective awareness, maintaining division, fueling battle-energy, and feeding the illusion that righteousness requires control.

This isn't new. Ancient Sumerian tablets speak of cosmic wars—galactic clashes that spilled into Earth's story. In some ways, we're still caught in the same energetic battle. It just looks different now.

As mythologist Joseph Campbell once said, *"Myths are public dreams, dreams are private myths."* The myths we're told—especially the ones cloaked in morality, nationalism, and God—can function like dreams we never wake up from. When those myths become collective obsessions, they form egregores that hijack personal truth and lock people into roles they never consciously chose.

Liberation begins when you become lucid in the dream.

But here's the truth:

You are MORE powerful than the narrative.

You are not helpless. You are not at the mercy of systems built on fear. Once you recognize the illusion, you can unhook from it. You can reclaim your sovereignty.

We'll return to this theme in Chapter 10 when we explore collective consciousness and the battle for your focus and frequency. But for now, let this plant a seed.

Not every thought you've been taught is yours.

Not every belief you've agreed to is benign.

The Gate of Illusions is about learning to spot collective distortions as well as your own.

The Soul Care Matrix™ and How It Came to Me

At one point in my life, I believed that blessings, miracles, and Divine orchestration belonged to a single tradition. That's what I had been taught... until I learned otherwise and started my own unbinding process. Through deep ancestral clearing using The Alexander Method® of Vibrational Sound and Energy Therapy, something *cracked open.* I saw, not just intellectually but *viscerally*, that Divine Intelligence was not confined to any *one* tradition.

This realization changed everything. It was the moment I understood that spiritual systems do not grant power. *They channel it*. If spiritual traditions offer structured paths for moving energy, then it's also possible to create frameworks that help people move through personal transformation.

That's exactly why I created *The Soul Care Matrix™*, a structured way to navigate the process of unbinding from illusions, realigning with personal truth, and embodying sovereignty.

Just like Ifá, Christianity, or any other spiritual system, this isn't about "the one right way." It's a guide, or a map... one that walks you through each layer of the unbinding process so that you're not wandering in the dark.

It aligns with **The Three Gates of Unbinding**: first, *seeing* the illusions (this chapter), then *releasing* (letting go of) them (Chapter 5), and finally, *stepping into full embodiment* (Chapter 6).

As we progress through the remaining chapters, you will see *The Soul Care Matrix™* in action. In the Resource section at the end of the book, you'll be able to access a template and examples of how to structure *your own* energetic flow through this framework.

Remember, fear keeps people locked in illusion. It keeps them from exploring the fullness of their intuitive gifts. It teaches them to fear what they don't understand, to demonize what doesn't match their doctrine, and to silence the parts of themselves that already know how to move energy in powerful ways.

The Gate of Illusions invites you to see beyond the label. To listen deeper. To question who taught you what to fear and "why."

To recognize that what you've been told was dangerous may actually be your doorway to freedom.

Chapter 4 Recap:

- Illusions distort our perception: they convince us to shrink, silence ourselves, and accept false limitations.

- The greatest illusion is separation from God. But Divinity was never external; it has always been within.

- The word "witchcraft" weaponizes fear, when it is simply working with energy.

- Religious traditions and spiritual systems are frameworks, not absolute truths. They offer structure for moving energy, but alignment is what matters.

- Ifá and Ori clarify this concept: while intermediaries can guide, personal connection to Divine wisdom is always accessible.

- Science and spirituality were never separate. Frequency is real, structured, and measurable.

- Many people live for the afterlife instead of engaging with life now. But true embodiment happens in the present, not in waiting for what comes next.

- Energy speaks louder than words. intuitive perception is real.

- The Soul Care Matrix™ provides a structured path for recognizing illusions, letting them go, and stepping into alignment.

Next: The Gate of Release

Now that we've uncovered the illusions, the next step is to untangle ourselves from them… to clear the interference, shift our perspective, and reclaim what has always been ours.

CHAPTER 5

THE GATE OF RELEASE

Unbinding, Surrender, and the Art of Clearing Space

There's a moment in every process of transformation where we stand at the threshold between what has been and what could be. The weight of the past, whether personal, ancestral, or even beyond this lifetime, lingers in ways we don't always recognize. It shows up in the body, in the patterns we repeat, and in the doors that never quite seem to open.

But *release*, or rather, unbinding from what has kept us tethered, is not about forcing something away. It's not about rejection, resistance, or cutting something off with brute force. It's about allowing what is no longer aligned to dissolve, to soften, to make space for what is truer.

This is the paradox of surrender. It is not passive, but deeply intentional. It is not giving up, but rather giving *over* to clarity, to truth, and to the intelligence of the soul that has always known the way forward.

When Letting Go Feels Like Losing Control

Many people resist the idea of surrender because it sounds like weakness. They fear that if they stop gripping so tightly... whether to a belief, a relationship, a fear, or even a version of themselves... they will fall apart. That if they let go, they will lose control.

But here's the truth: when we are clinging, we are already not in control. We are caught in the tension of holding on to something that is not naturally staying. Real freedom comes not from forcing, but from aligning.

There is a distinct difference between reactive resistance (fighting to hold onto what is slipping) and conscious surrender (choosing to allow something to shift so we can move more freely).

One of the most profound ways I've witnessed this process—both personally and professionally—is through The Alexander Method® of Vibrational Sound and Energy Therapy. This work has shown me time and time again how gentle, yet deeply powerful, the process of clearing energetic weight can be. Whether it is ancestral, emotional, or even rooted in experiences beyond this lifetime, the moment that energy shifts, everything else in life begins to realign.

What follows are several stories—mine and others—that demonstrate this process in action. Each one is a real-life example of what it means to unbind, surrender, and allow space for transformation.

A Debt, An Energetic Imprint, And an Unexpected Answer

One of the most impactful experiences of unbinding in my own life came through an energetic clearing that shifted something I had no idea was even there. I had a debt hanging over me. Not just financially, but energetically. No matter what I did, I couldn't seem to move the situation forward. It felt like something beyond just money was keeping me from resolving it.

During an Alexander Method® vibrational energy clearing session I did on myself, something surfaced. It was an energetic wound from childhood that I hadn't even realized was there. The pattern that was playing out in my financial life had been imprinted unknowingly by my father years ago, a moment that I had long forgotten but that my subconscious and energy body had stored.

The moment this realization landed, the shift began. And what happened next was something I couldn't have planned.

On the very same day, a book I had ordered—completely unrelated to what I thought I was working through—arrived in the mail. Flipping through, my eyes landed on a passage at the bottom of the page, describing, in detail, the exact kind of energetic injury I had just uncovered in my session!

This was confirmation, *not* coincidence.

Within days, the debt that had felt so impossible to move was resolved. It was never just about the money. In actuality it was truly about the energetic blockage that had been holding the pattern in place.

A Professional Seeking Clarity: When the Answer Wasn't What She Expected

For years, she had built her life around certainty. She had a structured career, a well-planned future, and an unwavering vision of what was meant to unfold. But when we decided to explore what vibrational sound and energy therapy would be like for her, it wound up revealing, *and thus her facing*, something she never anticipated: an outcome that would not exactly line up with her expectations.

She had spent years believing that if she remained determined, if she followed the right steps, if she simply *held on long enough*, what she deeply desired would manifest. She had navigated challenges before, times when outcomes weren't solely in her hands. But this was different. What was coming to the surface was the realization that the more determined she was, the more resistance she would be met with.

During our vibrational sound and energy therapy session, a past-life memory surfaced, which she agreed to explore. As we moved through the process, the memory didn't present as a direct answer, but more so as a feeling... one that lingered before she fully understood its weight.

At first, she tried to rationalize it and find a direct link between what she was experiencing in this life and what had come through in the session. But past-life imprints don't always reveal themselves in neat, linear ways. Sometimes, they arrive as emotions or as *echoes* of choices the soul once made. They can arrive as the quiet knowing of a path already walked. Over time, the more she sat with it, the more the pieces started coming together.

What she was determined to have in this life, the thing she was so *certain* she could make happen if she just held on, was tangled in something much deeper: A past-life imprint of loss, of an irreversible outcome, of a choice that had consequences beyond what could be seen at the time. And in that moment, she faced something she had never allowed herself to consider:

What if the very thing she was clinging to was not meant to unfold in the way she had envisioned?

The realization broke something in her.

For so long, she had pushed forward, unwilling to entertain any other possibility. But here, in this space, she allowed herself to feel what she had been unknowingly resisting: the weight of *surrender*. Not surrender in the sense of giving up. Not surrender as defeat… But surrender as a softening… a willingness to release the rigid hold on what she thought *had* to happen and instead make space for what *was* happening.

Was there grief? Yes. Uncertainty? Absolutely. But alongside it, there was something else: a deep exhale… a release of pressure she didn't even realize she had been carrying.

For the first time, she allowed herself to stop fighting. To stop forcing. To let go of the belief that her *will* was enough to override what was unfolding. She left that session not with the answer she had expected, but with a clarity she hadn't realized she needed.

And clarity, even when it arrives with grief, is still a gift.

Surviving a Cult and Releasing the Weight of Shame

There are stories that take years to fully understand. Not because the facts are unclear, but because the feelings attached to them are so layered and so tightly woven into identity, that it takes time & tenderness to even begin the unbinding.

For this client, leaving a high-control religious group should have been the end of the struggle...

But it wasn't.

Even though she had physically walked away, *something* still clung to her: A weight, an invisible force... something that kept her locked in a cycle of guilt and unworthiness she couldn't quite explain. She had done the work: counseling, introspection, rebuilding her life from scratch. But no matter how much progress she made, the shame remained. It showed up in her thoughts, her decisions, and even her body like an ever-present residue she couldn't shake.

During her vibrational sound and energy therapy session, a past-life connection surfaced. But at first, it didn't make sense. She was trying to find a linear explanation, trying to tie it to something in her current life.

But this wasn't exactly linear. Instead, it was energetic.

During the regression, a feeling emerged from her: a deep, overwhelming sense of hopelessness. Regret. Shame. A past-life imprint of something *devastating...* something that, in that lifetime, she had been *unable* to stop. And in this life, without realizing it, she had spent years trying to overcompensate for it. Trying to be "good," trying to be worthy, trying to atone for something she couldn't even name.

That was one of the main reasons why she had been drawn to the religious group in the first place, and also partially why she had stayed, why she had endured, why she had allowed herself to be controlled. Because somewhere deep in her soul, she believed she deserved it. Shrouded in the wound and residual energy of unworthiness.

However, there was a moment… the moment she saw what she had been carrying… wasn't hers to hold anymore.

Something shifted…

The moment she *forgave herself.* Not just in words, but on an *energetic level…* and the shame began dissolving. It didn't happen all at once. But over the following weeks and months, something astonishing happened:

The shame disappeared.

Not lessened. Not buried. Gone!

For the first time in her life, she REALLY felt free. Not just physically, but emotionally, spiritually, AND energetically! The weight she had carried for lifetimes… yes, lifetimes… had vanished! She later excitedly expressed to me, *"I can't explain it. I just feel… good. There is no shame. It's completely gone!"* And in its absence, something new had space to take root: Wholeness. Worthiness. And a life that was truly hers to claim.

The Shift from Searching to Receiving

Not all forms of liberation are emotional or dramatic. Sometimes the most powerful shifts happen when we simply stop trying so hard.

A friend of mine, (another mother), was struggling with trying to find her wedding ring. She looked everywhere! By the time she got to me, who knows how many places she had been before she realized she was without it. The stress was building, the tension was palpable, and she could NOT find her ring.

Although she seemed calm in the moment, I could tell she was nervous, frustrated and scared. I shared something with her I had learned from a book by James T. Mangan: a *switchword*, which is a single word that shifts mental states and taps into the subconscious.

The word was *"Reach."*

She repeated it to herself, with a curious look on her face, as if to say, *"Will this really work? I'll try it."* She continued to whisper the word under her breath so as to not forget it, and I encouraged her to feel where the word leads her instead of forcing it.

We said our goodbyes and I wished her well.

Shortly after she got back home, she called me:

"Megan! I found it!

It was on TOP of the refrigerator!"

She then remembered the very thing she was doing that made her put it on top of the fridge in the first place. She was both happy and blown away!

There was the ring she had been desperately looking for, sitting quietly in a place she never would have considered if she had stayed in effort mode.

That moment changed her. Not just because she found her ring, but because she found *her flow.*

I've experienced this, too.

I was on my way to an appointment and in a rush. However, before I left, I needed to grab an important document. I thought I knew exactly where it was. But when I looked, it wasn't there.

I checked the usual places. Checked them again. Still nothing. Meanwhile, the pressure was building. Someone else was waiting on it, and I clearly didn't have time for this!

The harder I looked, the more scattered I felt. And I know better! I know that kind of frantic energy doesn't open anything up. It just creates more fog and tension.

So, I stopped for a sec to gather myself. I called on my spiritual court. I asked for help. I got quiet. And sure enough... I felt the nudge.

Go back. Look again. Same place.

But this time, I slowed down. Let my breath settle. Let my body relax.

And there it was! Tucked just behind something that had blocked my view the first time. Not missing. Just... obscured.

That moment reminded me *again* that release isn't always about letting something go completely. Sometimes it's about releasing the panic, the urgency, the pressure... so you can finally *see*.

When Partnership Doesn't Match the Picture

There's a kind of unbinding that doesn't come from a single moment but from years of realizing that something you deeply value doesn't *always* move the way you expected it to.

For me, that showed up in marriage.

We've had seasons where it felt like we were speaking completely different languages. Not because we didn't love each other, but because our upbringings, our emotional wiring, and the ways we process life have always been different.

We didn't know what we were up against in the early years. The miscarriages. The pressure. The misunderstandings that weren't malicious, just deeply misaligned. I spent a long time feeling unseen. Not intentionally... but still.

We've grown a lot since then, and we're still growing.

There's no big, dramatic revelation here. What I've learned is that releasing the illusion of what marriage is supposed to feel like is a form of freedom, too.

Some days are easy. Some aren't.

We don't always move at the same pace. We don't always understand each other right away. But... we've stayed committed to the life we're building, AND to each other as *whole people*, not just roles.

I've been told I make it all look easy: mothering, marriage, self-employment. I don't share the hardest parts publicly, and I don't think I need to. That's not hiding. It's just knowing what needs to stay sacred.

What I *will* say is this: *we've had to let go of the idea that alignment means sameness.*

Sometimes I joke that we're like salad dressing – oil and vinegar. Completely different textures. But when we're shaken together *with intention*, something else emerges. Something flavorful that also holds.

The Fear of Power and Labels

Not everyone talks about it, but a lot of people are carrying spiritual fear. Not just fear of what's out there, but fear of what *might* happen if they *actually* own what they know.

Some are curious. They feel drawn to candles, cards, energy, ancestral work, etc... but no one ever showed them how to move through that world with grounding, protection, or clarity. So, they try a few things. They dabble... And when something backfires, or just feels too open, they retreat. Not because they're foolish, but because power, *without direction*, can take you somewhere you weren't ready to go. Especially when no one ever taught you how to trust your intuition *and* stay spiritually anchored.

Then there are people on the other side of the spectrum: folks who *want* to grow spiritually, but are still scared. Not because they've done something reckless, but because the fear is so deeply ingrained. They've been told not to trust themselves. Told to be careful what they "let in." Told that their dreams, their visions, their gut instincts might be dangerous *(this was me)*. So, they stay quiet. They keep their gifts to themselves. They watch their own wisdom rise up and then second-guess it.

And then there's a third group: People who know what they carry. Who've been walking with power for a while now. But still hesitate to show it. Because they're tired of being labeled. They don't want to be called "witchy." They don't want the whispers. They don't want to keep explaining that their practice is rooted in intention, alignment and reverence. So, they downplay. They stay low. They choose the path of least resistance, not because they're hiding, but because they're tired.

This gate is for all that.

The unbinding isn't just from old beliefs. It's from the fear of being seen fully. The fear of being misread. The fear of being "too much."

Letting go of the need to explain yourself.

Letting go of the pressure to prove you're doing it "the right way."

Letting go of the idea that your spiritual walk has to make sense to anybody else.

This doesn't mean moving recklessly. It means moving with clarity, integrity, and your own inner truth at the center. Not someone else's version of what's acceptable.

Power doesn't have to be loud.

But it does have to be yours.

These are small stories. Quiet moments. But they hold a powerful truth: *The mind can block what the spirit already knows.*

When we release the need to control through logic, we create space for guidance to rise. It's not about magic words or formulas. It's about softening our grip long enough to let truth surface.

The Soul Care Matrix™ And the Gate of Release

Letting go isn't just a one-time event. It's an ongoing practice! The Soul Care Matrix™ (SCM™) offers a clear, structured way to support the process of unbinding, surrendering, and realigning with your truth.

Within the SCM™, The Gate of Release is reflected across four key areas:

- **Initiation (Mind):** This is where you begin taking inventory of the belief systems, conditioning, and unseen forces that have shaped your reality (Chapter 4). Many of the patterns we cling to aren't truly ours. They're inherited, imposed, or absorbed over time. Recognizing that is the first step toward unbinding.

- **Alignment (Mind):** Here, you gain a wider vantage point. This is where contemplation, intuition, and discernment deepen... where you begin to notice what is truly aligned versus what has been held out of fear or habit.

- **Energy Hygiene (Body):** The body holds onto unprocessed energy. Clearing practices like vibrational sound and energy therapy, past-life regression, breathwork, or aura cleanses help loosen that build-up and restore flow.

- **Ritual (Body):** Release isn't just energetic. It also needs to move through the body. Movement, ceremony, prayer, offerings, and integration practices help ground what's shifting on the inside into your lived, embodied experience.

Tools For Letting Go & Moving Through the Gate of Release

As you navigate this gate, here are some supportive tools from the Soul Care Matrix™ that can help you stay grounded and open:

- **Energetic Clearing Practices** – The Alexander Method® of Vibrational Sound and Energy therapy, reiki, past-life regression, or meditation to help soften and dissolve long-held blockages.

- **Grounding & Protection** – Centering techniques to create a stable foundation as you let go of what no longer aligns.

- **Ritual for Release** – Writing letters, burning ceremonies, or intentional movement to create a physical shift.

- **Breathwork & Emotional Processing** – Somatic techniques that help your body move energy rather than suppress it.

- **Spiritual Alignment** – Calling on Divine guidance, practicing active surrender, and trusting that when something leaves, it's creating space for what's meant to come.

Letting go is an act of faith; one that honors your evolution and makes room for your next becoming.

Whether you're facing a financial block, a belief that's out of alignment, or an old energetic imprint that's finally ready to dissolve, the moment that tension clears, your life starts moving again.

That's the nature of vibrational healing. It doesn't push. It doesn't force. It aligns. And in that alignment, we remember what it feels like to move freely again.

Chapter 5 Recap:

- We explored what it means to release without resistance… to soften, not push.

- Letting go isn't always dramatic. Sometimes it's a quiet shift in how you see, what you carry, or what you're no longer willing to hold.

- Through real stories, we saw how emotional and energetic imprints can shape our choices until they're cleared.

- We saw how spiritual alignment deepens when fear of power, shame, or being misunderstood is no longer steering the path.

- Releasing isn't an erasure. It's a return to clarity of voice, energy, and self.

- Through breath, movement, stillness, sound, and truth-telling, we create the conditions for something more aligned to take root.

Next: The Gate of Embodiment

Once the weight lifts and the pattern no longer holds, something begins to open. What's been released doesn't just leave a gap. It creates space. And space, by nature, draws something in.

If we're not intentional, it gets filled with whatever's closest: old habits, familiar noise, new versions of the same thing. But if we pause... if we listen... that space becomes something else entirely.

A place for presence...

For rhythm...

For a way of living that reflects what's true, not just in thought, but in actual motion.

In the next chapter, we enter that space and begin to live from it.

It's the chapter where we land in the body. Where the spiritual becomes practical. Where presence becomes the practice. Where your alignment becomes less about ideas, and more about how you *breathe, walk, speak, and choose.*

Embodiment is not performative–striving to be perfect. Embodiment is all about allowing and actively engaging your inner truth to become your outer life.

Not once. But over and over again, in every moment.

THE GATE OF EMBODIMENT

Prelude: The Gate Within the Gate

If embodiment had a location, it would be the heart. Not just the emotional center. The energetic axis. The sacred middle ground where soul and skin meet.

Before we talk about rhythm... before we trace alignment across your practices, your lifestyle, or your day-to-day choices... We have to name this clearly:

Transformation doesn't happen in the mind. It happens in the **heart**. And if you try to skip over that, nothing else in this chapter will truly land.

The mind can analyze and the body can respond. But the heart is where change becomes **embodied** because it is the only place where your Divinity *and* your humanity truly meet.

This has always been known. Across every sacred tradition, the heart has been the gate:

- In Christianity, salvation is not intellectual—it must be *believed in the heart.*

- In Islam, the Shahada is spoken aloud, but it's truth must be held in the heart.

- In ancient Kemet, Ma'at does not weigh mind, behavior or titles. She weighs the heart.

- In Ifá, Eṣu—the Òrìṣà at the crossroads—governs choice, but not from the head. The turning point happens in the *body*. In the *moment*.

- In Catholicism, the sign of the cross passes through the heart.

- In Eastern traditions, mudras and bows begin and end at the center of the chest.

And now, even science speaks the same language.

The HeartMath® Institute has shown us that the heart doesn't just beat:

- It entrains.

- It calibrates the brain.

- It guides the nervous system.

- Its electromagnetic field stretches feet beyond the body and communicates before you ever say a word.

The first organ to form in the womb is the heart. The first rhythm we respond to is our mother's heartbeat. Before we know language, we know *resonance*.

So, embodiment isn't about belief. It's not about perfection. And it's definitely not about performing what you've learned.

Embodiment is about **coherence**. It's about living from the part of you that already remembers.

This chapter isn't asking your intellect to work harder. It's asking your heart to speak louder. It's asking your heart to guide you through presence.

The Soul Care Matrix™ (Continued)

Earlier in the book, we covered the first two layers of the matrix:

- **Initiation (Mind)**: The inventory. The inner confrontation. The uncovering of who and what has been running the show.

- **Alignment (Mind)**: The high-level vantage point. The unraveling of inherited patterns. The clarity of what's truly yours.

In this gate, we *now* enter the embodiment half of the matrix—grounded in the body:

- **Ritual (Body)**: The structure. The repeated physical practices that help anchor new frequencies.

- **Energy Hygiene (Body)**: The unseen field. The vibrational maintenance required to move clearly in the world.

This chapter will show you how embodiment lives inside both. How the smallest action, taken with presence, can realign your entire field.

Whether you realize this or not, embodiment doesn't just happen when you're meditating, journaling, or pulling cards. It happens in the carpool lane... at the grocery store... in the pause before you text back... It happens when you choose stillness over defensiveness. When you move with intention instead of reacting from survival. When you bring your spiritual awareness *into your nervous system*...into how you eat, breathe, speak, rest and respond.

The deeper you embody, the more you'll notice when something is off. It will be less mental and more visceral.

How does this look when it is actually lived?

The following personal accounts take you through moments when I became distinctly aware of how I was practicing embodiment.

My Path Found Me, and It's Still Unfolding

I spent years trying to force myself into a mold that was never meant to hold me.

"Just pick one thing."

That phrase echoed in my mind every time I tried to explain what I do, every time someone tried to box me in. It was always said with the best intentions, as if focus were the key to success... as if life were a straight line with a single destination.

But I don't move in straight lines.

I've never been the type to plant myself in one field and never leave. I move like a pollinator: sampling, integrating, weaving, expanding. I'm drawn to multiple things at once, not because I'm scattered, but because each piece feeds the whole. My way of creating, learning, and working isn't a distraction; it's how I'm designed to function.

For years, I tried to resist it. I tried to force myself into a structure that felt unnatural, thinking that maybe, if I just focused hard enough, or were disciplined enough, I'd finally become what others expected me to be.

But when I finally stopped fighting my nature, everything clicked.

I wasn't scattered. I was *orchestrating*.

Each thread of my work – teaching, performing, healing, writing, tuning – wasn't competing. It was harmonizing and working synergistically.

My violin business and my wellness business might look separate on the surface, but in reality, they are both about frequency, resonance, and alignment.

- **Violin is an external sound.** Performance, vibration, artistry... the frequency of music moving through air.

- **Wellness is an internal sound.** Healing, energy tuning, alignment... the frequency of the body and spirit coming into resonance.

It's all vibration. It's all resonance. Vibration Over Everything!

And the moment I embraced this, my entire perspective shifted.

I was never meant to follow a linear path. I was meant to spiral, weave, and integrate. I was meant to build a life where everything I touch is connected, even when it looks separate to others.

And once I embodied that truth, I stopped looking for permission to move the way I was *always* meant to move.

The Cost of Seeking Outside Yourself

For so long, I searched.

I reached outward for guidance, for signs, for something outside of myself to tell me I was on the right path. I thought if I could just find the right book, the right teacher, the right moment of clarity, then I'd know for sure.

But seeking can become a trap. There's a fine line between learning and outsourcing your power… between receiving wisdom and placing authority outside of yourself. The moment you default your power to something external, you create a leak in your energy field.

In that crack is where uninvited participants can step in.

This isn't to spark fear or to scare you, though It's an energetic reality. Nonetheless, it's one of which you're in control.

The more you resonate with doubt, fear, or uncertainty, the more you attract energies that thrive in those frequencies. This is how people get manipulated, how they fall prey to false teachers, how they find themselves tangled in spiritual systems that deplete them rather than empower them.

Energy is currency. Where you place your attention, your belief, and your devotion is where you invest your power.

When I fully understood this, I knew I had to seal those leaks.

I had to become the authority in my life.

The Mosquito Barrier (A story of frequency, feedback, and the realization of I Am)

I had a life-changing experience while in Pennsylvania for my Master Skills certification in the Alexander Method® of Vibrational Sound and Energy Therapy.

For a full week of training, we were at a lake house and cottages. Along the lake, the shoreline wasn't soft. It consisted of grey and black rocks. There was no sand. Just layers of stone meeting the water.

It was October, which meant the air was crisp, and normally by then, mosquitoes were out of season. The first couple of days were spent doing deep energetic work. Tuning each other and getting tuned ourselves. About mid-week, we were given solo time—an entire day for integration. To be by ourselves, take a walk, go to the water, journal, rest, etc.

No one told us exactly what to do. We were supposed to follow what we felt.

The day before, I felt a quiet nudge to go practice something I hadn't done before—not cleansing or grounding, but protection.

Energetic protection.

So on our integration day, I decided to give it a go.

I had always used prayer or intuition in the past, but I hadn't deliberately practiced building a protective energetic field. This time, I was being guided to try it. Not with words. Not for show. But from inside.

With self-talk pressure to "create content," I tried to record the moment at first, to document it and maybe teach from it later.

I tried to document–TWICE! But both times I tried, the environment gave me IMMEDIATE feedback.

The first time, I made my way down to the rocky beach and walked toward an area that looked like a good spot to sit. As soon as I put the phone aside to make myself comfortable, there it was– a huge dead bird carcass. What appeared to be the carcass of either a crane or a heron. Yeah… that big.

I had never seen anything like it on that beach.

That was my first "No."

The second time, I found a different rock on the very edge of the lake and got ready to record. I took a picture of the cottage, and a selfie, but before I could even really settle, the water suddenly got very wavy, and water started splashing up on me, right where I was sitting.

There were no boats. No wind. Just odd, splashing waves that seemed to appear out of nowhere.

I didn't need a third try.

I got up. Put the phone away and took time to make peace with what I then knew needed to be treated as sacred, and I wouldn't fully get it if I was "performing" or distracted.

Eventually, I went back to the rock, without my phone. Just journal and pen, & sat quietly.

I set my intention, closed my eyes, and started to breath slowly, rhythmically and with depth.

While enmeshed in breathing, I got the nudge again to open my eyes.

That's when it happened.

Mosquitoes began to gather.

A lot of them.

And it didn't make sense—it was October near the Poconos. They shouldn't have been there, at least not en masse like they appeared!

I could feel myself start to tense.

I kept asking myself: Do I move? Should I swat them away? Should I hold my breath?

I began to feel a bit afraid that if I even breathed, they'd come closer.

But underneath all the mental chatter, I kept hearing one thing:

Be still.

So I did that. I stayed still.

I focused my energy and I built a field that domed like a shield.

I didn't pray aloud or ask for anything.

I just held the energy of stillness and protection— intentionally, for the first time.

While my eyes were open, I noticed the mosquitos would only come to roughly an arm's length before they would drift in another direction. I heightened my senses to see if I could detect wind or a draft that may be swaying them.

No wind.

No draft.

One by one, they would approach and would drift.

I watch it repeatedly… one after another, sometimes two or three at once.

None of them landed on me. They didn't even come near me.

They didn't touch me at all!

That's when the tears came.

Not because of the mosquitoes. Because of what I realized in THAT moment.

A hymn I grew up hearing in church came back to me— "On Christ the Solid Rock I Stand…"

But this time, it landed differently.

It wasn't about someone outside myself.

It was me!

I Am the rock!

I Am the one I was looking for.

I Am the Christ in this moment—anchored, grounded, protected!

It all hit at once.

Not as an idea, but as something I could feel in my body! It was truly visceral!

I got the lesson and gave tear-filled gratitude to God and my spiritual court for the lesson and ensuring the space was held for me to experience that.

I started writing in my journal, and THEN the mosquitos started landing once the exercise in energetic protection was complete and I redirected my focused attention.

Completely full from the experience, I got up and began making my way back to the cottage to reflect and integrate even more.

And then, just like the other time before when I'd visited this same lake for a previous training, I looked down… and spotted a clear quartz crystal sitting among the rocks.

This was the THIRD one I'd found on that beach. That beach has no sand. It's all stone. You don't just find quartz there.

When I told my teacher about it and showed her the crystal, she said she had never found a clear quartz crystal there in all her years of living on that property.

But every time I had come—every time I reached a new level of clarity or integration—I found one.

This was number three and I knew what it meant.

That moment wasn't about mosquitoes.

It wasn't even about protection.

It was about embodiment.

It was specifically about learning how to hold my own frequency with such intention and presence that nothing misaligned could touch it.

That was the lesson.

Again, it was not something I could have recorded.

It had to be lived.

When Embodiment Begins at Home

Marriage will show you where your mind says "I'm fine" but your heart says otherwise.

It's one thing to talk about alignment in theory. It's another thing entirely to try living it *under the same roof with another human being*, day after day, season after season.

For my husband and I, it hasn't been one tidy story. There have been beautiful seasons and *very* hard ones. There have been moments of deep connection… and… long stretches where it felt like we were speaking different languages, living at different temperatures.

We didn't know what we were up against at first and found ourselves abruptly side swept by deviations in expectations. Even though we love each other, for a while, we hadn't yet learned how to name the energy moving between us in a healthy and beneficial way.

There were times I wondered if I was being gaslit—not through intentional cruelty, but through genuine mismatch in perception.

There were other times where I felt the ache of being unseen, even by the person who I thought knew me best.

And yet—beneath all of that—there was still **something steady**.

Not perfection.

Not effortless harmony.

But a *shared commitment* to the life we were building together, even when our frequencies weren't syncing easily.

Learning to live sovereignly inside marriage has been some of my *deepest* embodiment work.

It taught me that sovereignty doesn't always mean separation. It taught me that you can hold your own frequency even when closeness feels out of reach. It taught me that love is not always about fixing or forcing—it's oftentimes about keeping your own heart open *without* handing it over.

I used to think that thriving in marriage meant never feeling misunderstood. Now, I know that thriving sometimes means choosing to stay present even when understanding isn't instant. It means recognizing when the dissonance isn't a threat, but simply a signal instead. Where dissonance becomes an invitation to come back into alignment with *yourself first*, before reaching for resolution outside of you.

Our marriage isn't perfect. It's a living, breathing agreement to grow—individually and together. Some seasons, we flow like music. Some seasons, we sound more like two violin strings, both out of tune, trying to find harmony.

Either way, the work begins in the heart. *Always*... in the heart. True embodiment doesn't skip the places that feel messy. It moves through them with tenderness, clarity, and enough sovereignty to stay rooted while still reaching out to regain connection.

When Ritual Becomes Reality

It started with powder in my shoes. Not just any powder— **road opener**... A sacred Hoodoo tool, placed with intention.

In the middle of miscarriage—still cramping, still bleeding, still holding onto the rainbow braids I had woven into my hair as a prayer for life— a door opened.

And somehow, even in grief... I said *yes*.

The music festival had been whispering to me before I truly believed it could be something I would experience. I had dreamed of it quietly, never fully saying it to others aloud... And then seemingly out of the blue, the invitation came.

I was still miscarrying. I was still unraveling from the inside out. And yet, I dusted the inside of my shoes with road opener. I lit a seven-day candle for clarity, grounding, and the courage to show up as I was.

After receiving the invitation, I only had a few days to prepare. The difficulty of the music was *far beyond* anything I had ever learned!

I did NOT feel ready!

Not emotionally.

Not technically.

But... I was *aligned*.

So I held on to the realization that I *was* there, so I was *supposed* to be there!

I followed the conductor like scripture.

I leaned in to ask my stand partner quiet questions.

I studied. I observed. I listened.

I gave everything I had—with the equipment I had at that moment.

I showed up green, breath tight, body still processing loss—but I showed up fully.

When it was over, it was quite a bit to process everything that led up to that moment.

I sat. Violin resting. Heart buzzing. Feeling most alive, in awe and wonder of what I just experienced... Letting it sink in that I had *just done* something I used to think I wasn't built or qualified for.

I hadn't just shown up. I stretched. I poured. I allowed myself to receive.

After that event, for years, invitations to return to perform in the festival kept coming!

Not because I was exceptional in performance–*far from it*–It was because of resonance.

That first performance with the festival wasn't just a gig. It was a turning point, where grief made room for expansion, and where I stopped needing to *feel* ready in order to *be* ready. It was where I embodied the truth that I didn't have to wait for validation to belong.

I just had to keep showing up with my whole self!

Beyond First Impressions

Embodiment doesn't stop at home. It has to travel with you into public spaces, shared rooms, and around unfamiliar energy. One of the most tested places is the pressure to make a *first impression*.

There's this idea that how you're perceived in the first few seconds will define how people receive you. It's a widely held belief that you need to lead with polish, presentability, and palatability. Especially as a Black woman, especially in professional or predominantly white spaces, *especially* when you carry something unconventional in your energy.

And yes, I've learned how to move through certain spaces with care. Yes, I know when I'm entering a room that's dominated by a particular tone—refined, tight, manicured, cautious…etc.

I've worn the gowns. I've dressed for the part. But even when I do… I don't leave myself at the door. Because here's what I've come to understand:

I can't control how anyone sees me.

I can only control how I carry myself.

I'm not just talking about posture or tone of voice—I mean energetically.

I'm in control of the energy of how I feel about myself in that moment…what I'm honoring… whether I'm in touch, or shrinking, or standing fully in my frequency.

If my presence—the fullness of it—causes someone to make a snap judgment or turn away, maybe they weren't aligned with me to begin with. Maybe that's not a loss, it's protection.

I don't dress to impress at all. I don't tailor my voice to match what someone else will find most "digestible." What I wear, how I speak, the energy I lead with—it's all for personal alignment, and not necessarily approval.

There's a difference between adapting and abandoning. And for a long time, people taught us women, and black folk, to do the latter.

Be nice. Be soft. Be small.

Don't offend. Don't overdo it. Don't be too much.

But now?

I can enter a room in a gown, sit at a table, speak with intention, offer my ideas, represent my work—and still hold a cultural cadence in my voice. I can still speak with a rhythm that reflects where I come from. I can still let my face express joy, confusion, and connection. I can still tell the truth, even if my vocabulary doesn't sound like theirs.

That's not code-switching. That's me consciously practicing resonance with integrity.

It means I know how to be aware of a room without erasing myself inside it. I don't dilute. I don't contort. I walk in already holding the frequency I want to be met with.

From an energetic perspective, first impressions aren't about performance or being demonstrative. They're about holding and honoring your presence. That's an inside job and not an external display.

When you show up anchored in your true presence, not the one for show, the people who are meant to resonate with you will feel it—whether they can name it or not

Moving Through the Divide

There are moments when embodiment meets the road—literally.

I remember a moment recently where I was headed to a performance in a part of the state known for its quiet hostility. It wasn't loud or overt. But the undertones? Palpable.

There are regions where your skin feels like it enters the room before you do, and your spirit knows it needs to be twice as grounded.

So as I drove, I found myself calling on protection. Not from paranoia—but from ancestral memory. I consciously called in my guides and Divine coverage. I don't do this out of fear. I do this because I've learned how to read the room before I even arrive.

I know what I carry, so I know what it means to move through the world as a Black woman. The projections. The assumptions. The coded threats wrapped in civility. I don't really subscribe to the belief that Black women are "the most disrespected"—not in my sovereign body, not in my spirit. But I do carry awareness. Because awareness is power. And embodiment means moving with both reverence and readiness.

I arrived safely. Once inside, I could feel the weight of historic ritual in the air—traditions over a hundred years old, carved out for a very specific class and kind of people. The architecture, the decor, the formalities… they all echoed a legacy. A lineage of access preserved through something other than what I was holding.

—

Later that same weekend, I played for another event. Same state. Different energy.

This one was rooted in African American tradition—another 100-year-old lineage, shaped by those who had been locked out of spaces like the first one.

It was powerful and poignant. And comparing the energy of the two, I could feel how both spaces were, in their own way, performance.

They both contained rituals born of legacy and longing. One preserving access and the other fighting to prove we belonged.

And yet… both were still tethered to systems that no longer reflect where we're going.

Both were shaped by tribal codes—spoken and unspoken— that still tell people who they need to be to belong.

As I sat there—instrument in hand, body anchored, heart open—I felt the contrast from a place of clarity and not judgment.

As a people, we are still performing. We're still adapting to projections. We're still aligning with the energy of survival in spaces that ask us to shrink, prove, or polish ourselves into acceptability.

But we don't have to stay there.

At some point—*and maybe that point is now*—there comes a moment when we remember:

We are not divided.

We are not fragments.

We are not bound to the projections placed on us by systems we never consented to.

We are ONE.

Even if the world has tried to make us forget.

And so ... in both places, I played.

Not from fear.

Not for approval.

But from *embodiment.*

Because that's what sovereignty sounds like in motion.

The Drum I Was Meant to Carry

I remember the ache. The kind of longing that doesn't shout, but simmers instead.

I was growing up in a beautiful family—one I was proud of. But still, somewhere in the quiet corners of my childhood, I felt small...Overlooked... Unseen in ways I didn't know how to name.

And more than anything, I longed to belong.

Not just in the way of fitting in, but the kind of belonging that has depth. Or the kind that feels like a drumbeat you've always known. It feels like a rhythm that meets your body before your brain can translate it.

I wanted sisterhood (*I had three older brothers*).

I wanted rites of passage (*African Americans sometimes lack this*).

I wanted to be part of something that had roots older than the soil I stood on.

I wanted culture that felt chosen, not just handed down by circumstance or conditioned history.

As a Black woman in America—like so many of us—I didn't grow up knowing what indigenous tribes I came from either on the motherland or this stolen one.

I didn't know what dialect my tribal ancestors spoke or what foods were passed down before they were forced into scraps.

I didn't know which foremothers survived assault, which forefathers disappeared under papered ownership.

I didn't know. And that "not-knowing" created a gap I didn't have the tools to fill.

I wanted to carry a different flag.

I wanted to speak a language that wasn't wrapped in colonizer breath.

I wanted to move in rituals that weren't borrowed from television or stitched together from fragments.

I remember wanting to join African dance troupes.

I wanted to wear fabrics that told stories.

I wanted to sit in ceremony with women who remembered who they were.

But the external guidance I trusted said "no."

Before I even went to college, I expressed interest in joining a few cultural sisterhoods—rites-based organizations that carried that tradition of belonging.

And my father told me flat out: Don't do it. "You already have a family. You don't need that."

Even the one I called my angel—the one I trusted with so much of my becoming—dismissed it. He didn't just warn me. He judged the people who did it. And I remember shrinking back, because even when you don't agree, when someone you respect names something as unworthy, it leaves a mark.

So I didn't go.

I didn't join.

Instead, I started listening to the quiet rhythm I'd always heard in my own chest. Over time, I noticed that the people I was most drawn to were the ones marching to their own drum too.

Maybe that's always been my path. Maybe the belonging I longed for wasn't something I was meant to inherit. Maybe I was meant to **become** it.

Maybe I was meant to signal a new rhythm… to model what it looks like to thrive *without* the cultural markers and ready-made rites… to create a life of depth and spirit, even without the structure.

And that's what embodiment has become for me: Living fully, without waiting for approval. Being anchored, even without the banner. Knowing that I can still move with reverence, beauty, and power… Even if the tribe I come from doesn't have a name. Even if I had to become the drum I couldn't find.

Heaven Was Never the Goal

There's a strange distortion that takes root when you've been taught that earth is temporary, and heaven is the real home. That this body is fragile, sinful, and fleeting…

but the spirit—that's what matters. That this life is a test, and the best thing you can do is *pass*.

But something about that always sat sideways in my body. Even when my mind was trained to accept it. Because if I believed the goal was heaven, then what was I supposed to do with this life? What was I supposed to do with this body? With this breath? With this beauty? With this ache?

That belief shaped more than my theology. It shaped my nervous system. It shaped my relationship to joy, pain, truth, self. It made me afraid to be here fully. It created fear around wanting too much, or resting too deeply. It made me fearful that if I relaxed into pleasure, into sovereignty, into being... I might miss the mark. I might disqualify myself.

Because the real prize was somewhere else, right? After the struggle. After the suffering.

After this...

whatever *this* was.

This mental framework teaches you to postpone embodiment. It teaches you to delay your arrival, and to live on the edge of your own life... trying not to get too comfortable, too confident, too loud, because any moment of "too-muchness" might send you spiraling.

And yet...

The more I came home to myself... the more I sat with my own body, my own breath, my own memory, the clearer it became.

I began to understand clearly that this is not a rehearsal. This is no warm-up. This is not a low-grade trial to see if you're worthy of something better later.

Life now? This *is* the miracle. This *is* the mystery.

And your soul chose this—not to escape it, but to *inhabit it*.

Fully.

Fully inhabiting this life means feeling the ache, the joy, the longing, the heartbreak, the friction of being in skin. It means recognizing and feeling the pull of duality. It means accepting the privilege of touch, sound and stillness.

To bypass all of that…

to rush past it…

to be so consumed with where your soul will go *after*…

that you forget what it came here *to do*–is to miss the entire point.

So here's where it clicked for me:

If I am constantly aiming to be with God later, I will overlook the ways Source is trying to *BE with me now*! – Through my breath. Through my body. Through the way my heart pulses in rhythm with life.

The Divine doesn't ask you to wait. Instead Source asks you to *wake* and to remember that heaven isn't a reward. Heaven is a state of resonance.

And it begins here.

Right now.

At this moment.

In the miracle of being alive—still tethered to breath, still held in a vessel that allows you to feel, become and embody.

You don't have to wait for death to become whole. You don't have to wait for heaven to meet God. You don't have to leave your body to live your truth. The sacred is not only found above. It is folded into *everything*!

The ones who taught you to fear the body? To fear the earth? To fear your own power?

They were afraid of something they couldn't control or didn't fully understand. This isn't to find fault in them, but to remind you that once you remember that you are not waiting for arrival, and that you've already arrived? You become *unshakable*!

You stop trying to earn what you already are.

You stop *striving toward* Source, and start *living as it*!

Chapter 6 Recap:

In this gate, we moved beyond ideas and into lived experience.

We explored what embodiment actually looks like. Not as something polished or distant, but in the real, textured moments of life.

Through eight personal reflections, we touched different aspects of what it means to live sovereign and unbound:

- **Just Pick One Thing:** the call to honor a non-linear, multidimensional path instead of shrinking into a single identity.

- **The Cost of Seeking Outside Yourself:** the reminder that searching for external validation leaves cracks in our energetic field, and how reclaiming our own center is the real protection.

- **The Mosquito Barrier:** a lived moment of energetic sovereignty, where intention, stillness, and presence created a real, measurable shift in the environment.

- **When Embodiment Begins at Home:** the work of holding energetic sovereignty inside a relationship. Not through separation, but through honoring personal resonance during seasons when mutual understanding felt harder to reach.

- **When Ritual Becomes Reality:** stepping into expansion even in the midst of grief by using ritual as a bridge into embodied readiness for closure and moving forward.

- **Beyond First Impressions:** choosing energetic presence over curated appearances, and trusting that resonance speaks louder than performance ever could.

- **Moving Through the Divide:** witnessing how rituals of belonging and social structures are shaped by cultural memory, and choosing awareness without absorbing inherited projections.

- **The Drum I Was Meant to Carry:** honoring the deep longing for ancestral rootedness, and learning to become a signal of sovereign belonging without waiting for external validation.

- **Heaven Was Never the Goal:** Letting go of afterlife preoccupation to reclaim presence in the body, by recognizing that true connection to Source happens here, not someday, not somewhere else.

Each story added another layer… building the architecture of what embodiment really asks of us, which is presence, not perfection.

From this gate forward, embodiment is no longer theory or something you aspire to.

Embodiment is something you live, breathe, and return to again… and again… and yet again, but with your whole self intact.

Before You Move Forward

You've just moved through a lot. You saw what embodiment can look like… through confusion, breakthrough and through those quiet spaces where nobody else can really walk it for you.

Maybe, somewhere along the way, a part of you stirred. Maybe you thought about moments in your own life that haven't had a name until now. Maybe you remembered the times you held yourself together in ways no one else ever saw.

You don't have to figure it all out today.

You don't have to turn it into a project.

But before you move on, maybe give yourself some space.

Maybe ask:

- Where has embodiment already been showing up in my life, even if I didn't call it that?

- What parts of me have been waiting for me to notice?

- Where am I still holding back, and what would happen if I didn't?

You don't have to rush the answers or even get them "right." Simply let them sit with you like seeds finding their way into soil. Here's the truth... you've already been walking this path longer than you realize. So what's next? It's You... letting more of what's *already true* take up space.

PART III

LIVING UNBOUND

"I didn't break free. I just stopped shrinking.
And that was enough to change everything."

There wasn't a single moment when the sky cracked open and said, "Now. Now... you are free." It was quieter than that. Slower. More cellular. It came when I stopped asking for permission to be what I already was. It came when I realized nothing needed to *snap* in order to shift. It came when I stopped trying to squeeze my spirit into the shape of someone else's comfort... and started moving from my own inner rhythm instead.

Living unbound doesn't always feel revolutionary. Sometimes it feels like the absence of tension. Like clarity where there used to be static. Like breathing without an apology.

This is the part where you stop rehearsing and start *living* the truth you've been remembering all along, and for that, you will need more than insight.

You'll need alignment.

No rules or performance.

Only alignment as *a way of being* that meets you in every step... every breath, and every choice you make next.

CHAPTER 7

THE ART OF ALIGNMENT

I wasn't even looking for anything big that day. Just flipping through a beginner book, half-paying attention, when something caught my eye. *Place your third finger on the A string. Make a D. Watch the open D string wake up.*

It sounded simple enough. I wasn't sure it would actually work. But I wanted to see. So I picked up my violin, found the note, and played it. And sure enough, the open D string started to ring.

It wasn't dramatic or loud. Just a soft vibration, almost shy at first, like it had been waiting for the right note to find it. And when it did? The whole sound literally expanded.

It didn't happen by force or pushing more. The sound just BECAME fuller... rounder. Alive.

I didn't know the science yet. I wasn't fully aware of differential tones, or sympathetic resonance, or how two notes perfectly in tune can make something new appear between them.

All I knew was that when the pitch was right, the open string answered back. And when it wasn't, the open string stayed silent.

This experience taught me something I've never forgotten:

Alignment isn't something you force. Alignment is something you feel. It is something that wakes up inside when you're close enough to the truth.

That's what we're stepping into now.

Remember, we're not chasing perfection or muscling our way forward, which may be contrary to what you're used to or have been told is necessary to get ahead. We are now learning *how to listen* for what's *already* trying to resonate with us and how to find our way back when we drift.

Resonance: What the Body Knows Before the Mind Catches Up

Resonance isn't fancy. It's not mystical. It's natural. It's how energy moves when it isn't fighting itself. It's not just violins or music. Once you notice resonance, you start seeing it everywhere.

You see it in how buildings are put together—how the edges have to meet cleanly or the whole structure wobbles under pressure.

You see it in dentistry—how teeth aren't aligned just to look good in a smile, but because a proper bite distributes force evenly, keeps everything working the way it's supposed to.

You see it in nature—how birds flying in formation aren't just following a leader, they're catching the same current, adjusting by fractions of an inch to stay in the flow.

In science, this phenomenon is called **coherence**—when your brain, body, and heart are in a synchronized rhythm. The HeartMath® Institute describes it as a measurable state where your physical systems operate in harmony, creating clarity, ease, and resilience.

But coherence isn't just physical. It's energetic, emotional and spiritual.

You *know* it when you feel it. When the "yes" in your spirit is matched by the calm in your body. You *know* it when the action you take doesn't just "make sense." It *feels* right. Like it belongs. It feels easy. Not laziness. Not giving up. Just ease.

And just as importantly, you know when it's missing. You can tell when you feel that ache in your chest after you said "yes" to something that's a "no." Or that fog in your head when you try to talk yourself into what your soul hasn't co-signed. Or even that low-level tension that buzzes beneath everything—even the things that look right from the outside.

Coherence doesn't mean every part of your life is perfect. What it means is that every part of *you* is in agreement about your next move.

THAT'S alignment.

It's the difference between *forcing* your way forward and *flowing* into the next right step with clarity. It's a living relationship. You notice when you drift. You notice when you start fighting the current again. And you choose—without panic, without shame—to come back.

Here's where it gets even *MORE* fun. When things are really aligned, something wild happens. The energy doesn't just move easier. It moves *BIGGER*!

It's not just that friction disappears. it's that the whole thing starts carrying itself forward, creating momentum… like you caught a wave you didn't have to create.

You do less. And somehow more happens.

In physics, they call this phenomenon **constructive interference**: two waves meeting at the right place, at the right time, and making each other stronger without trying.

But you don't have to know the science to feel it.

You know it when the conversation leaves you energized instead of drained. When the "yes" you gave keeps opening doors without you having to knock them down. When the thing you said "yes" to keeps feeding you instead of bleeding you.

Real alignment doesn't just ease the struggle. It multiplies your reach. It takes what you already are... what you already carry... and lets it move farther than you could've pushed it alone.

Micro-Adjustments: The Real Work

Most people think alignment is about making huge life decisions. Quitting jobs. Leaving relationships. Starting something new. And sometimes, yes, alignment calls for a bold move. But mostly, it starts out smaller than that. It's a posture... a breath... a single pause before you respond.

It's choosing to eat when your body says it's hungry, even if your calendar says work through lunch. It's saying "let me get back to you" instead of people-pleasing on autopilot. It's noticing that you're holding your breath again, and letting your shoulders drop an inch lower.

Most realignment happens so quietly you could miss it if you're not paying attention. These aren't grand gestures. They're course-corrections, which matter much more than you probably think! Alignment is about building the sensitivity to feel when you've slipped a little... and the *self-trust* to do something about it early... before the drift becomes a disconnect.

Sometimes it looks like pausing mid-conversation and softening your tone. Sometimes it's stepping outside for a minute because your energy's getting scrambled and you know better than to pretend it's fine. Sometimes it's leaving the email unsent until your spirit clears, instead of pushing words out of frustration and calling it productivity.

Little things.

Small turns back toward yourself.

Most people don't see them. Most people don't even feel them until it's been days or weeks and everything inside them is buzzing with static. But when you start living inside your own coherence, you notice faster. You start hearing the off-key hum sooner. You catch the drift at the whisper stage instead of waiting for the scream.

The beauty lies in this:

The more you *practice*, the less friction there is between noticing and adjusting. It stops feeling like a crisis. It just feels like being honest:

"This isn't resonating."

"This isn't breathing right."

"This needs a shift."

Before you know it, you make the shift without apology or theatrics or dragging yourself through shame or guilt for needing a retune.

Oftentimes, people may fall into a trap of "trying to heal" thinking that alignment is some golden state you lock yourself into once you're "healed enough." That's not how alignment works. Instead, it's a living *relationship* with your *own* frequency.

It asks and requires you to *stay close to yourself*, to *listen* when your body hums *differently*, to trust that noticing the drift isn't failure, and self-mastery in action instead.

At this point, you might be thinking, *"But what if I don't feel anything? What if I've tried this before and nothing changed?"*

That's real. And it's not because you're broken. It's because noticing alignment, trusting it and *living inside it* is a **practice**. It is a building of sensitivity over time.

If you've spent *years* bracing against life, tuning yourself to survival instead of resonance, *of course* it might feel unfamiliar at first. *Of course* it might feel like you're guessing sometimes. It doesn't mean alignment isn't real. It means your body is remembering how to hear it again.

Which also means, it's okay if that remembering feels awkward, slow, or imperfect.

Keep trying. Keep staying in the conversation. Stay close enough to begin noticing the subtleties, which will become more clear as you practice.

Hearing Yourself Beneath the Noise

The challenge isn't always finding alignment when everything's quiet. It's finding it when life gets noisy–When the texts are piling up, the deadlines are breathing down your neck, and the world outside is throwing static into every corner of your day—

THAT'S when the real practice shows up.

Let's face it. It's *EASY* to stay tuned when the room is still. It's easy to feel centered on a retreat… a walk through the woods… a perfect morning where no one's asking anything from you.

But what about the middle of a Tuesday afternoon when you're tired and your phone won't stop buzzing and you're pulled in six different directions? What about when the world feels like it's humming a different frequency, louder and louder, trying to pull you out of yourself?

If alignment is the goal, **resonance** is the language it speaks. It's not just a metaphor. It's literal.

In physics, resonance happens when two frequencies match. Not forcefully, not through domination—just naturally. One begins to hum, and if the other is built to respond, it hums back, like the example I shared from my own experience at the beginning of this chapter.

This is why tuning forks are used in orchestras, energy work, and even medical practices. Strike one, and another tuned to the same pitch will begin vibrating in response—no contact necessary. No coaching. No convincing. Just resonance.

The same thing happens to you.

You know when you enter a space and your body says *yes*. Or when someone speaks a truth, your spirit has already known, and you feel your whole chest respond before your brain has the words? That's the resonance. That's alignment registering on a level deeper than logic.

You've felt the opposite, too. You've nodded in conversations that drained you. You've smiled through situations that shrunk you. You've agreed to plans that made your stomach tense and your breath shallow.

The trick isn't in avoiding every dissonance—it's in becoming so familiar with your own frequency that you can feel when you're off center, and know how to return. It's about knowing how to feel for your own signal underneath the noise. That hum you learned to recognize. That sense of *this fits* or *this doesn't fit,* which neither screams nor demands—it just stands steady... Quiet, but unshakable.

Sometimes it takes a breath to find it. Sometimes it takes a step back. Sometimes it's just a simple question in the middle of the swirl:

*"Is this moving me **toward** myself or **away** from myself?"*

No judgment.

No drama.

Just noticing.

You start remembering that alignment was never about escaping life, but instead living it while awake. Breathing inside it fully. Choosing, moment by moment, to stay close to your own resonance even when everything around you is vibrating in a different key.

That's the work now.

Alignment isn't about getting every step perfect. It's about staying in relationship with yourself, moment by moment, and noticing when the hum gets louder or when it fades.

Alignment nudges you to return when you drift, to adjust when you need to, while trusting that resonance isn't something you earn, but instead, something you uncover, over... and over... and over again.

It's an *art* that you *live*. Not a finish line that you cross.

The more you live it, the more you remember:

You're not here to wrestle life into submission. You're here to participate in it fully.

Chapter 7 Recap:

- **Alignment is a living relationship**, not a rigid state you achieve once.

- **Resonance is natural and measurable**: It can be felt in the body, in the breath, and in the way life expands when energy is moving cleanly.

- **Coherence happens when your mind, body, emotions, and spirit move in the same direction**, creating ease rather than friction.

- **Small micro-adjustments matter.** Realignment isn't about huge moves. It's about noticing and tuning sooner, with less drama and more grace.

- **Constructive resonance amplifies your energy.** When you're aligned, you don't just conserve energy, you multiply it.

- **Alignment is an art.** It asks for presence, responsiveness, and a willingness to return, again and again, without shame.

What's Next?...

You're not just aligning for the sake of feeling good at the moment. You're doing so because your life, the story you're here to live, needs the real you in it.

Not the version of you shaped by survival. Not the one sculpted by someone else's expectations. The true... breathing... resonant... *you*.

The next step in this work is reclaiming the story you've been living inside of by asking whose voice has been speaking through you, whose patterns you've been carrying, and how you can choose, from here, to write the next chapter differently.

Alignment is what makes it possible. However, reclaiming your narrative is what makes it *real*.

As you begin to rewrite, you might mistake chaos for passion or urgency for importance, or noise for momentum. That's okay. It just means your nervous system is re-calibrating. Give it time. Rewriting is a practice of remembering, noticing and returning to Self.

CHAPTER 8

RECLAIMING YOUR NARRATIVE

Story Is the Original Technology

Long before satellites… before search engines and social media algorithms… before scriptures were canonized, before we even had written language—there was story. Story was the original technology. It was how we transferred knowledge before books.

It was how we remembered the medicine. How we made sense of suffering. How we held the sacred.

Story was the drumbeat that held time. The firelight that made sense of shadows.

The bridge between the ancestors and the unborn.

Even now, beneath all the noise of modern life, story is what shapes us.

We think we're moving through timelines. But really, we're moving through stories—some inherited, some chosen, some still being written in real time.

Some of the biggest wars in history were fought over stories– about who God is and who we are. Who belongs. Who should rule? Who is right? Who must be silenced.

We forget this.

We forget how many of the "truths" we live by started as someone's *story*–A framework. A metaphor. A meaning-making map.

And the most powerful stories are the ones we never think to question.

Think about what shaped you:

- The bedtime tales. The Bible verses. The parables.
- The mythologies—both ancient and modern.
- Generational loops disguised as family pride or shame.
- The Sunday sermons and the secular mantras.
- The zodiac memes.
- The "what - you're - supposed - to - do – by – age - 30" timelines.

So much of what we call reality is really *narrative architecture*.

If you don't recognize that, you'll think your life is fixed... instead of something that can be *re-authored*.

Story doesn't just describe life. Surprise! Story actually creates it! It gives life shape. Direction. Context. Desire. Belonging.

Story tells you what to expect and what to avoid. What to dream and fear. It tells you how people like *you* are supposed to behave. What's possible. What's permitted.

Story is how the world first taught you who you were. Before you had memory... you had a story.

And if that's the case, if we are *truly that impressionable*, that programmable, that energetically responsive to story, then it makes perfect sense that the most powerful thing you can do for your evolution is not just to learn something new... but to *tell something new*.

You see, when people say "change your life," they often mean change your behavior.

But real change—lasting change—starts with changing the *narrative input*. It's changing the signal you're sending to your system… the story your *body believes* it's living in.

Yes, your nervous system responds to the story.

That's how you can hear a sentence and suddenly your breath shortens, your stomach tightens, or your eyes water. That's how a single childhood memory can echo into adulthood like it just happened yesterday. That's how a myth can shape a culture for thousands of years.

Story is sensory. It's emotional and cellular. Story shapes your *mind* AND imprints your *body*.

So this chapter isn't just about rewriting the plot of your life. This chapter is focused on reclaiming the original code. And understanding that *you*, just like the myths and scriptures and legends that shaped you, are a living, breathing technology of your own.

Your new story can recalibrate.

Your new story can reorient.

Your new story can speak its way back into alignment.

—

There comes a moment—quiet, unassuming—when the story you've been telling yourself starts to feel too small. Not because it was all a lie. Not because you fabricated your memories or imagined your struggles. It feels too small because the version of the story that got you here… is no longer the one that can carry you forward. And if you're honest, it probably never quite fits.

Reclaiming your narrative isn't about denying the past. It's about giving yourself permission to narrate it from the place you *now* stand—clearer, wiser, and more connected to your own voice than the noise that shaped you.

The Voice You Were Told to Use

For many of us, the stories we inherited were whispered before we had the language to question them. We were taught what it meant to be good, to be worthy, to belong. We absorbed expectations like oxygen—silent, invisible, essential. We learned which parts of ourselves to showcase, which to suppress. And slowly, unconsciously, the voice of our story was handed over to others.

Maybe it sounded like:

"You're the strong one, you don't cry."

"You're so mature for your age."

"You're lucky to even be here, don't mess it up."

"This is what success looks like."

"Don't ask for too much."

"Be humble. Be grateful. Be quiet."

Even if the words weren't said aloud, the rules were made clear. Fit the mold, or forfeit the love. Assimilate, or be cast out.

So we performed. We adapted. We became fluent in survival, silence, and in performing a version of ourselves that made others more comfortable. But silence and survival aren't the same as sovereignty. And eventually, the body starts to revolt against a story it never chose.

Meaning Is Not Fixed

We treat words like they're final. We treat stories like they're fossils. But language is not a museum of meaning. Language is a living thing. It breathes, it shape-shifts, it evolves with us.

What meant one thing at age ten may mean something completely different at age forty. Words that once felt like comfort might later feel like a cage. The phrases you used to avoid, may now actually hold your liberation.

Even sacred texts have been rewritten. They have been translated, edited and reframed. These texts didn't originally arrive as leather-bound King James Bibles with gold foil edges. They were spoken, retold, and reinterpreted. They were passed through generations, re-coded in different tongues and reshaped by different ears.

Yet... we hesitate to do the same with our *own* stories.

We hesitate to revisit what we've labeled "truth." We fear that if we change the meaning, we're being dishonest. We wonder if reclaiming something, by rewriting it with a different tone or letting it carry new frequency, means we're abandoning what actually happened.

But meaning is not a static thing. Meaning, too, is a frequency, and like you've seen in the last chapter, frequency responds to presence. Meaning changes based on *who you are now*, not just who you were when the story first landed.

So when you look back on the breakup, the loss, the moment you were silenced, the years you spent inside someone else's definition... what would it mean to revisit that moment through today's frequency?

Not to erase what happened but instead, to let it stretch and breathe, while offering your body a new interpretation. Even the most concrete-seeming things... (words, memories, identities) ... they are made of "air."

And so are you.

So if you find yourself rehearsing old language... or if you catch your thoughts returning to narratives that no longer feel true... ask yourself gently:

- Is this the only way this story can be told?

- Is this still the meaning I want to carry?

- Or am I ready to translate this moment into something new?

Meaning expands when you do, and your story is ready for more space.

The Unraveling

Rewriting your story starts with telling the truth—not necessarily to others, but to yourself.

- What part of your current narrative feels out of sync with your inner knowing?

- Where have you been performing instead of living?

- What truths have you tucked away to maintain peace with others, while disturbing your own?

There is no formula for this reckoning. Sometimes it shows up as a quiet sadness. A subtle discomfort. Other times, it roars through a breakdown or an unexpected moment of clarity. It doesn't always announce itself with language. Often, it arrives as an ache. A refusal to keep pretending. A deep need to be seen as you actually are—not as who you've been edited down to be.

You Are the Author Now

To reclaim your narrative is to step back into authorship. It does not mean you erase the past. It means you choose how to interpret it. It means you stop allowing other people's discomfort, projections, or limitations to dictate your meaning.

It means you ask questions like:

- What if the parts I was most ashamed of were actually signs of my depth?

- What if the "too muchness" I was told to tone down was actually my power?

- What if I didn't have to justify or explain the parts of me I've always known?

Reclamation begins where justification ends. When you stop trying to make your life story make sense to people who were never meant to understand it, you create room to make peace with it yourself.

You don't need to confront everyone who got it wrong. You don't need to call a family meeting or write a public blog post. Sometimes the most sacred shifts happen quietly... in your own body, in your own breath... when you decide to stop dimming and start living.

Resonance Is the Rewrite

Here's where it gets nuanced. There's a difference between lying to yourself and telling a new story.

This chapter isn't about bypassing or pretending your past didn't happen. It's not about repeating affirmations you don't believe or trying to "positive-think" your way into a new timeline. It's about choosing words, thoughts, and beliefs that *resonate* with *where you're going*, not just where you've been.

The Law of Resonance teaches us that your frequency determines your experience. Not just your thoughts, but your felt, embodied frequency. And language? It carries frequency.

At first, shifting your story might feel like you're being dishonest. Saying "I am safe" when your nervous system is still bracing. Saying "I trust myself" when you've spent years second-guessing. Saying "I am loved" when your current relationships don't reflect that yet.

But you're not lying. You're tuning.

You're choosing a new frequency and letting your body learn how to hold it.

And yes, it might feel clunky at first. Like trying on clothes that don't quite fit yet. But the more you speak in resonance with where you're going, the more natural it becomes. You're not faking confidence. You're practicing it. You're not pretending to be whole. You're remembering that you already are, and letting your cells catch up to that truth.

When you change the inputs... your words, your rituals, your beliefs... you change the output. Because resonance always responds to Source. *Always*.

So when it feels foreign, don't panic. You're not being fake. You're shifting fields. You're recalibrating your story from survival mode to sovereignty. From performance to truth. From noise to signal. Let your nervous system learn the new rhythm. Let your tongue form new patterns. Let your story find its footing.

You don't have to *feel* the words fully at first. You just have to mean them enough to begin.

From *"To"* to *"For"*

Sometimes, the narrative shift starts with just *one word*.

It sounds almost too simple to matter. But the moment you ask, "Why is this happening *for* me?" instead of "Why is this happening *to* me?"— the entire frame of your story moves.

It moves you from victimhood into vision. It moves you from powerlessness into possibility. It moves you from being at the mercy of life to being in *conversation with it*.

That one word—*for*—opens a door your nervous system didn't even know it could walk through.

This isn't about spiritual gaslighting or forcing meaning onto pain. It's not about pretending every experience is a blessing wrapped in trauma. But it *is* about reorienting your gaze so you can become a participant in your life again, and not just a passive recipient of it

The Role of The Reticular Activating System

The Reticular Activating System, or RAS, is the heat-seeking part of your brain that filters reality. It decides what information to bring into focus based on what it thinks you care about. You're constantly feeding it cues (through your language, beliefs, and intentions) about what to look for.

So if you say, "Nothing ever works out for me," your RAS goes out and collects proof to support that.

If you say, "I'm always behind," your brain will ignore the wins and highlight the delays.

But if you shift the narrative... just a word, a tone, a tiny opening... your RAS re-calibrates and responds differently.

It starts looking for evidence of growth, provision and alignment. It begins to confirm what you've chosen to believe *on purpose*.

This is where energetic sovereignty meets brain science. You're not just telling a new story. You're *training* your biology to support it! When your brain and body are moving in coherence with your intention, your entire frequency begins to shift!

This Is Where It Got Real for Me

I have lived on both sides of this thing. Multiple times.

There was a version of me—devoted, sincere, born-again—who was trying to live "right," trying to stay in alignment with the version of holiness I'd been taught to embody. I gave. I praised. I tithed. I fasted. I stayed in worship. But underneath it all ... was *lack*.

I didn't know it at the time. I wouldn't have called it that. But it was there—quiet and shaping everything. I was doing all the "right things," but the energy underneath them was desperation. Grasping. Trying to get God to move, trying to get proof that I was okay, that I was covered, that my sacrifice was enough. I called it faith, but the undercurrent was fear.

Later, as I expanded beyond Christianity—still holding the essence of Christ, but allowing myself to explore ritual outside the walls of the church—I experienced the same thing. I burned the incense. I said the words. I anointed, I honored, I listened. And sometimes things shifted. Sometimes they didn't. Not because the ritual was ineffective, but because I was still operating from the same old lack frequency—just in a different outfit.

See, your Reticular Activating System doesn't just respond to the words you say. It responds to the *frequency you carry*. So if you're speaking abundance, but your body is humming with unworthiness, your RAS will go searching for evidence to confirm the *real* frequency—the one running underneath.

I had to learn that.

The effort I was putting out was real. The rituals were real. The intentions were good. But the stories I was telling—about who I was, what I deserved, and whether I could trust the outcome— were still being shaped by lack.

Once I started moving the lack out of the driver's seat, everything began to respond differently. My body. My results. My sense of timing. My expectations. When I gave from fullness, instead of scarcity... when I praised from peace, not panic... when I asked for clarity from a place of alignment instead of collapse... things started to shift. Not because the rituals changed. But because *I* did.

That's when I saw the real power of storytelling, not just as a mental practice—but as an energetic one. What you believe, what you say, what you expect—it all lives in your frequency before it ever shows up in your reality. And your RAS will faithfully organize your life around the signal you're sending.

So now, when I speak something into being—when I claim it, pray it, align with it—I pause and ask:

- What frequency is under this?

- Am I speaking from fullness, or fear?

- Is this desire grounded in resonance, or in reaching?

The story only works the way I desire it to if the energy behind it is clean.

Words, Intention & Coherence

Let's talk about the space between sound and meaning.

Words don't operate in a vacuum. They're carriers. They hold vibration, and... they also hold *intention*. Intention isn't always loud or obvious. Sometimes it hums beneath the surface, shaping the resonance of a message even when the words appear harmless.

Consider the work of Dr. Masaru Emoto. His water experiments showed how different frequencies—spoken words, music, even thoughts—affected the crystallization of water molecules. Beautiful, harmonious sounds produced elegant, symmetrical crystals. Harsh, angry sounds produced chaos in the crystal formations.

But here's what always made me pause: we don't know the intention behind those sounds. We don't know what energy lived in the hearts of the musicians, the speakers, the researchers. We only saw the effect.

So it begs the question: *Can something sound beautiful but still carry dissonance?* Can someone say all the right words and still leave you feeling pierced?

Yes. Absolutely.

Here's why. Coherence isn't about surface-level sound. It's about alignment between the intention, the energy, AND the delivery.

You can mask lack with a smile. You can dress manipulation up as encouragement. You can string affirmations together and still feel like you're lying—because the words aren't vibrating in alignment with your core.

I've seen this play out in the most ordinary of ways. In my own home actually. Sometimes my husband will say something— maybe offhand, maybe factual—and on the surface, there's nothing wrong with the words. He doesn't mean harm. But how it *lands* in my body... It feels bad. It stings. And suddenly, I'm responding from the wound, and he's looking at me like I'm overreacting.

But here's the nuance: he didn't *intend* to hurt me. And I didn't choose to be hurt. We were both operating from two different resonant fields.

So then what? Who owns the impact? Who adjusts? Where does sovereignty come into play?

Here's what I've learned:

Sovereignty doesn't mean you numb yourself to how things land. It means you become *aware* of how things land, and then learn to trace the thread back to your own resonance. Your own filter. Your own story.

Because even if someone says something carelessly... even if the tone is off, the delivery jarring, the intention murky... you still get to choose how you digest it. You still get to decide what meaning to assign to it. You still get to discern whether that frequency belongs in your field.

That's not about bypassing real harm or pretending everything is love and light. It's about understanding that we are constantly in a dance with frequency. Constantly exchanging. Constantly navigating not just what is *said*, but what is *felt*.

Pause:

This is where the narrative gets slippery.

Sometimes the story you're choosing to live into, will look like delusion to other people.

They'll say, "Be realistic." "That's not what's happening." "You're making things up."

But what they call delusion might be vision. It might be faith. It might be a frequency your body can feel before the external world catches up.

So yes—be discerning. Be honest. Don't use storytelling as a way to avoid reality.

But also: don't let other people's inability to perceive what you're carrying cause you to abandon it. You are allowed to live inside a narrative that's aligned with where you're going—even if it hasn't fully materialized yet.

As long as intent is pure.

As long as the energy is coherent.

As long as the frequency is true.

You're not manipulating yourself. You're tuning yourself.

Chapter 8 Recap:

- Story is the original technology, which is woven into our cells, shaping our reality before we ever speak a word.

- From sacred texts to bedtime tales, we inherit stories long before we realize we're allowed to question them.

- Reclaiming your narrative doesn't erase your past. Instead, it gives you agency over the meaning it holds now.

- Language is frequency. Intention matters. The story only resonates when energy and words align.

- The difference between lying to yourself and speaking a new truth is often just unfamiliarity.

- Even sacred language evolves. Your story is allowed to shift, stretch, and speak again, because you too, are shifting, stretching and growing.

- Meaning is not fixed. You have the power to translate your experiences through a new lens of resonance and coherence.

- Rewriting the story starts in small ways: one word, one phrase, one breath at a time.

- You are not here to perform a narrative that doesn't fit. You are here to remember, reshape, and reclaim your own.

You've reclaimed your story. Not just the words, but the weight of it. You've stretched meaning and let old truths unravel. You have given yourself permission to speak something new.

Now comes the part where you live it out in the open and with other people. This is the time to live it inside systems that still expect you to bend.

So now, the question isn't whether the world will shift, *because it already is*. The real question is whether you'll contort to meet it, or stay grounded in what you have recently uncovered as truly real.

However, let's be clear. We're not pretending things won't potentially shake you. Staying unbound is knowing what holds and matters, even when "life gets to lifing."

In the next chapter, we look at what it takes to move through collective change without losing yourself in the noise.

We'll look at how to stay clear, how to stay internally connected and how to keep your signal steady, even when everything else moves or changes. Again, we're not reaching for perfection here. Just presence, discernment, and just enough truth to keep your footing when everything else is shifting. That's where we're headed next.

CHAPTER 9

THE PATH FORWARD |
SOVEREIGNTY IN A
SHIFTING WORLD

There's always something." –That's a phrase my dad used to frequently say when stuff would come up and be a wrench in the plan or an interruption causing an accomplishment being delayed.

There seems to *always* be some crisis... some broadcast... some collective drama designed to make you forget what you know. Its purpose is to persuade you to grip tighter, breathe more shallow and second-guess your own center.

And... if you're not careful, trance works.

But this moment... it doesn't feel like the previous old ones. It's got a different kind of weight to it. Like something's splitting—but not just breaking down. Something is loose *and completely undone*. Something ancient... Something we didn't even really know we were still holding.

We're witnessing in real time, old narratives fraying. Old roles are slipping. And the ways we've been taught to survive (*by aligning with fear, or by hardening ourselves*) aren't cutting it anymore.

Coherence feels much more urgent now. But remember, not the kind you perform. Not the *"hold it together"* kind. The urgency is for the kind that shows up in your body. The kind that whispers when your nervous system wants to scream. The kind that pulls you back when the world tries to scatter you again.

What steadies you probably won't get applause. It might not even get noticed. But you'll feel it... in your gut... in your breath... in your chest... in spaces you no longer shrink to fit. It's the part of you that stays grounded, even when the ground doesn't. It's what steadies you simply because you let go of the idea that everything has to be fine. It only needs to be aligned.

Side by Side, Seeing Differently

We are living in a time where what looks like "truth" is often propaganda, and what gets celebrated as righteousness is sometimes just spiritualized manipulation.

You can see it playing out in real time: politics dressing itself up as faith. Dogma disguised as morality. Collective trauma repackaged as identity.

The programs are running—colorism, sexism, racism, individualism—and they're louder than ever. But you don't have to keep feeding them. You don't have to stay hooked into the narratives that are designed to pull at your empathy, to twist your intuition into compliance.

Because manipulation is not always loud. Sometimes, it moves quietly. Soft-spoken. Internalized. It teaches you to brace. To expect harm. To doubt yourself unless fear says it's okay to believe otherwise.

I remember sitting with a family member one afternoon. Same space. Same sunlight. Same background noise. But it felt like we were in two completely different realities.

They sat alert, scanning for threat—interpreting every movement, every shift, as a sign of danger. Their body was locked in a loop of defense, even though nothing was happening. I watched it play out in real time. The tension. The vigilance. The story being told in their nervous system.

And me? I felt still. My body wasn't registering danger. I wasn't in denial. I just wasn't tuning into the same broadcast.

That moment taught me something: *we can share physical space, but we don't always share energetic reality.* And we don't have to!

Personal power isn't found in resisting fear with *more* fear. It's found in noticing what you've been conditioned to expect... and then *choosing* differently. Choosing to stay in your *own* frequency, even when the world around you is vibrating with anxiety. Choosing to believe your body when it tells you you're safe. Choosing not to outsource your perception to someone else's programming.

This is how personal power starts to return. Not instantly or all at once, but in a series of small, quiet refusals.

The Soul Care Matrix™ and the Reclamation of Choice

When I developed The Soul Care Matrix™, it was never just another framework. It can serve as a legend to the map your soul has been walking all along. And... it applies across the board.

It's not locked inside one religion. It's not reserved for the most enlightened. It's encoded into the design of your being.

When you understand The Soul Care Matrix™—when you learn how to circulate your consciousness through its components—you begin to refine what you believe. You become clearer about which parts of your identity were handed to you, and which ones you actually chose. You stop outsourcing your alignment to systems that were never built to hold your full humanity.

There's a point when correcting your self-concept stops feeling rebellious and starts feeling like coming home. Like remembering something your spirit always knew—but your programming made you forget.

You're not just here to belong to God. You're here to *reflect* God. Not in a distant, abstract way, but instead, in a real, living and breathing way as energy-filled, flesh-covered, personified Divinity in motion.

You were never meant to *chase down* what *already* lives in you! Remember, you *are* Source—expressed through your being, not separate from it! The more you remember, the less you search. The more you live it, the less you explain.

Once that knowing settles in, your relationship to everything else does too!

The Lie of "Going It Alone"

One of the fears that surfaces when you start honoring your own rhythm is the idea that you'll have to walk this thing by yourself. That choosing alignment will cost you connection, or that clarity means disconnection.

Sometimes doing things differently *does* create space. Sometimes people gradually fall away or even apart. But sometimes... *you stay*, which becomes its own practice in itself.

There were seasons in my marriage where our frequencies didn't match. I was moving through a lot—energetically, spiritually—and it felt like we were vibrating in different directions. Not in direct conflict. Just... distant. Like I was becoming more of myself and wondering if there'd still be space for that version of me in our togetherness.

But I didn't leave. And I didn't fold.

I stayed and let it *s t r e t c h* me...

I had to learn how to hold my own energy without requiring him to match it. I had to learn how to gradually soften again without disappearing. I had to learn how to listen without always editing myself to keep the peace. None of this was easy. But it wasn't always isolating or isolated either. It was definitely work.

Sacred work. Quiet work. Diligent and determined work. Work that changed the atmosphere in our home before it ever changed the language.

This proved to me that there is a way to grow *inside* connection... redefining and re-creating it.

That's something I wish more people said out loud. That leaving isn't the only portal to freedom. That some of us are here to learn to stay. How to remain rooted *and* resonant. How to walk with people we love while still answering the call to evolve.

And no, I haven't done any of this alone.

There's been help. More than once. More than one kind.

The Earth Angel who showed up right before my father passed and stayed throughout that agonizing transition... He cracked something open. But he wasn't the only one.

There were therapists—four, to be exact. Each one met me at a different version of myself. Each one helped me ask different questions, and stay with myself a little longer.

There were doctors who didn't just talk *at* me, but listened. Doctors who didn't *pathologize* the whole of me just because *one* part was tired.

There was sisterhood. The kind that lets you unravel out loud. Who lets you vent unfiltered. The kind where vulnerability is raw, and can hold the ugliest aspects of all of you. The kind that doesn't flinch when your truth shifts. The kind that holds you accountable without holding you hostage.

And there's my steadfast husband. Who could've walked. Who had every reason to check out completely at some point. But he didn't. He stayed. We both did. Even when we didn't know what version of us we were staying for yet. Even when the shape of our connection was still being re-formed.

Support hasn't always looked clean, easy or even comfortable. Sometimes it looks like distance. Sometimes it looked like tension, like friction that refined me. And sometimes it even looked like silence that gave me space to hear my own voice. It even looked like awkward laughter at the kitchen sink because neither of us had the words yet—but we were still trying. Every piece of it helped me stand stronger in who I am.

That's what nobody tells you.

Living sovereignly doesn't mean going it alone. In a world pulling you in a hundred directions—trying to hijack your focus, your values, your voice—sometimes the most sovereign thing you can do is *not* isolate. It's letting yourself be supported by people who help you stay clear. Who don't distort your signal. Who keep you close to yourself.

Sovereignty isn't disconnection. It's discernment.

It's the slow realization that not everyone stretches you thin. Some people stretch you open.

Start with the "Yes" You CAN Give

It's easy to talk about alignment in theory. It's harder to live it when everything around you is uncertain. And still—you do. One decision at a time. One moment at a time.

Sovereignty isn't about mastering the chaos. Living sovereignly is about learning how to move when the map dissolves. Because at some point, the map you were handed starts to fall apart. And you have to learn how to move anyway.

That's where the Soul Care Matrix™ comes in—not as a formula, but as a legend. A way of interpreting your life with compassion and clarity when everything familiar starts to fall away.

I didn't know what sovereignty was when I prayed that prayer…

I had just been THROUGH it and couldn't seem to catch a break—graduated with my Bachelors, no job, still grieving my father, suddenly engaged, and then broke up a year later, caught in the ripple effects of 9/11. I was working in finance, trying to hold it together, had to move due to the break up, my car died, had to buy a new car and pay for school out of pocket. The terms of my finance job transfer weren't clear. I was making significantly less money. Shortly upon arriving at the new location, I interviewed for and accepted a new contract position with an engineering firm—the very same day the finance firm's twin tower headquarters was hit.

It's easy to look back and name a single decision as the turning point. But it wasn't just that one day. It was everything that came before it. Every choice I'd made trying to figure out adulthood. Every shift I ignored until I couldn't. Trying to find footing in an industry that felt nothing like home. Grieving silently. Market collapse. Working hard. Surviving. Eventually unemployed for almost two years. Saying "yes" to things that didn't align, simply because I didn't yet know how to ask for what *did*.

By the time the financial services door slammed shut, I was already standing at the edge. It wasn't just a change. It was an apex. A collapse. A burst. And somehow, in that breaking open, there was room for a new prayer to rise.

But it wasn't just about the economy. Something in me was shifting. I was starting to want something else. Something not tied to systems that could collapse. Something no one could take away.

I said it out loud one day—quiet but clear: "*I want to do something that no one can touch. Something that nothing can strip from me. I want to do something with my violin.*"

My roommate heard me. She paused and said, "That's so wild… Alex just told me there's a violin teaching position open at a music store. It pays $16 an hour."

I remember how the air changed. The way my arms chilled with goosebumps. She wasn't even considering it for herself. Had no interest. She just passed it along. And somehow, it was exactly what I needed to hear.

I didn't have a degree in music education. I hadn't studied pedagogy yet. I was nervous. But I said "yes."

That "yes" turned into the career I love and live now! That shaky, unconventional beginning paved the way for a life that exists outside the traditional lines. A life I could've never scripted…one that keeps evolving with me. It lit something in me that has never gone out!

That's the thing about sovereignty. It's not about controlling everything. It's about listening—to your body, to the moment, to the invisible threads pulling you somewhere new.

―――――

This chapter of your life isn't about surviving the world, but instead, building a life the world didn't teach you how to imagine. We're focusing on stewarding your energy with care, clarity, and most importantly, courage… courage to let your stewardship make room for what's next, and hear yourself through the noise.

That's the thing about living sovereignly in a shifting world. Sometimes it starts with a moment of refusal. A decision not to keep chasing what doesn't fit. A willingness to try something that feels small but true. It may not look like certainty. It may not look like the scripted "success." It looks like a mustard seed of self-trust. A quiet frequency that says: *Start here.*

Sometimes it's teaching your first student with a borrowed method book and an old music stand. Trusting that the rest will come.

It's in the way you breathe through what breaks. The way you say yes to what feels small but alive. The way you keep showing up—even when the path is unpaved and no one is clapping.

Chapter 9 Recap:

- Sovereignty lets you choose your experience without needing others to validate it.

- Living from a corrected self-concept is an act of remembering. The shift comes when you stop trying to be understood and start truly living in alignment.

- Discernment, not distance, is what protects your path.

- Aligned purpose often begins in quiet, imperfect beginnings.

- The Soul Care Matrix™ helps you see your path clearly, even when the terrain feels uncertain.

What's Next?

You're still here! And you've accomplished a lot! You have begun reclaiming your rhythm, not just for your own peace, but as *preparation...*

The next step isn't just about how we live within ourselves. It's about *how we live WITH each other*!

In the final chapter, we turn toward the collective: The illusions that divide us. The intelligence that connects us. And what it truly means to build something whole.

CHAPTER 10

THE COVENANT OF UNITY – RECLAIMING OUR COLLECTIVE DIVINITY

This chapter actually began forming on the heels of the so-called attempted assassination of, at the time, former President Donald J. Trump. The coalescence and timing of it all is fascinating, but not surprising. It feels familiar. Like a loop I've seen before, a pattern that replays itself over and over, wearing different clothes, new language, but the same root frequency underneath.

There was a time when I might've been shocked. But now, I turn inward. Not to escape. But because I've learned to recognize the real battleground—it's not out there. It's in us. Between us. Beneath the surface of all the commentary and clamor is a deeper fracture that's been growing for generations.

Not just between political parties or religious camps or racial identities. But between souls. Between the sacred remembering of who we are to each other—and who we've always been.

We've covered so much in this book. You've done the work to reclaim your inner compass, to release false narratives, to stand in your body with full awareness. You've remembered the truth of your own frequency.

And now, we zoom out.

Because the path of personal sovereignty was never just about you. It's how you move in the world. You're a signal that ripples through every room you enter. The way you carry yourself becomes part of how we all remember who we are to each other and with others. Inside systems that are still shaking, still wired to divide. It's about how your remembrance contributes to a larger restoration—one that reconnects us to our collective Divinity.

The Conditioning of Fear

We have been taught the world is dangerous. That if you're different, you're a threat. That if you don't fall in line, you're a liability. We're taught to fear what we don't understand.

Turn on the television, and you'll see it—the programming. The subtle, daily reminders that shape public perception: that a young Black boy in a hoodie is a threat. That a pregnant Black woman is irresponsible. That a person worshiping differently is suspicious. That a person asking questions is dangerous. All designed to reinforce one thing: *fear*.

Redlining wasn't just about real estate. White flight wasn't just about neighborhoods. These were energetic movements rooted in fear—fear masked as logic, as preservation, as policy. And now, Christian nationalism has taken that same fear and dressed it in scripture. Turned it into dogma. Weaponized it with a flag.

Fear of hell has become more real, more potent, more politically motivating than the very real harm being done to women whose bodies are legislated through the stroke of a pen. People have mistaken obedience for love. Patriotism for truth. God for the empire.

And the most dangerous part?

We buy into it. We absorb it. We carry it into our homes, into our communities, into our conversations. We silence ourselves to keep the peace. We contort our knowing to fit the mold. We reject our Divine instincts to avoid being labeled or left out. And slowly, we start to believe the lies are safer than the truth.

We mistake control for care. We mistake fear for faith.

"Fear leads to anger. Anger leads to hate. Hate leads to suffering." —Yoda

It's not just a cinematic line. It's a map. A mirror. A sobering observation of the cycles we keep repeating.

So much of the suffering we see—personally and collectively—didn't start with hate. It started with fear. Fear of difference. Fear of loss. Fear of power slipping out of our hands. And when fear metastasizes, it recruits anger to do its bidding. Anger, unintegrated, solidifies into hate. And hate... hate always extracts something. It never stops taking.

But here's where we slow the spin...

Hate may demand sacrifice, but *love* invites offering.

Let's name the difference.

Sacrifice isn't inherently harmful. It can be sacred. Conscious. An offering made in love, for alignment, for purpose, for care. People sacrifice sleep to complete a dream. They sacrifice sugar to restore their health. They make sacrifices in their careers to nurture a home. They even sacrifice time to serve something bigger than themselves. In ancient traditions, sacrifices are part of honoring cycles and energy.

But fear distorts sacrifice. Fear makes it transactional. Conditional. Fear makes sacrifice a performance under pressure rather than devotion. That's when sacrifice becomes suffering— when it's pulled or extracted from us instead of poured out from within us.

True, unconditional love doesn't coerce. It doesn't extract. It doesn't need a transaction to feel satisfied.

Fear-based systems require proof, performance, and penance. They want you to bleed a little to show you mean it.

However, love—when it's real—doesn't feed on sacrifice. It receives what's given freely. It honors what's offered without manipulation. It doesn't measure devotion by how much you've lost. True love recognizes the sacred in what you *choose* to give, not what's been *taken* from you.

The ascended Master Teachers modeled *THAT* frequency. Not just through what they taught, but through how they lived: Yeshua. Ausar. Buddha. The Magdalene. Orúnmìlà. They reflected the face of God not to elevate themselves, but to remind us: this is what's possible.

They lived what they believed. They didn't need to dominate to lead. They didn't need to manipulate to teach. The power they carried came from embodiment.

They were examples of self-mastery—fully human and fully aligned with Source. Their lives were reminders, not exceptions. They showed us that integration, not separation, is the way back.

Over time, even their stories were reshaped. Co-opted. Used to build systems that centered fear instead of freedom. But the truth is still intact, if we're willing to look past the distortion. These master teachers didn't come to create hierarchy. They came to mirror our own capacity.

That kind of love does not fracture—it restores. It calls us back into integrity. Back to Source. Back to each other.

Coherence Without Compromise

Here's the thing we're not taught loud enough:

You don't have to abandon your unique essence to be part of a unified field.

Unity isn't sameness. It's coherence. It's the frequency that emerges when each person is vibrating in alignment with their truth, *and* able to hold space for others to do the same.

But we've been sold a lie that unity means silence. Compliance. Being palatable. Being small. That's not unity. That's energetic erasure.

Real unity holds complexity. It honors nuance. It invites truth and tension to sit at the same table.

That's why we must re-humanize each other. Not through policy alone. Not through hashtags. Not through grand gestures that don't touch the roots.

But through presence. Through listening. Through becoming the kind of person who no longer sees someone else's sovereignty as a threat.

We start by preserving what is sacred—not just within ourselves, but in each other. Because if we lose our empathy, our creativity, our wonder, our capacity to connect beyond surface difference... we've lost the thread.

And make no mistake: there *are* forces invested in that loss. Energies that feed on division, manipulation, distortion. Entities and egregores that hijack belief systems and rewire them to serve control.

We've seen it. We're living in it.

When the language of love—Jesus, soul, heaven, truth—gets twisted into weapons... when Christianity becomes synonymous with nationalism... when grace becomes a gimmick... we know the veil is thin.

But even here, love is stronger.

The Soul Care Matrix™ exists not to replace spiritual systems, but to return you to your own. It's a compass. A framework. A way to navigate this dimension without being devoured by it. It helps you recover your mind without losing your heart. It reminds you that sovereignty doesn't mean isolation. And unity doesn't mean submission.

It means remembering.

Remembering that we are God, in motion. Not omniscient. Not all-powerful. But *deeply* sacred and directly tethered to the force of creation and all of creation itself. We are living, breathing, incarnate reminders that Divinity isn't just up there, or over there, or reserved for a chosen few.

It's *here.* In you. In me. In all of us.

Soul Technology in the Age of Simulation

We are living in a time when hard technology is evolving faster than most people can comprehend. Artificial intelligence, automation, and machine learning are no longer future concepts. They are here! Shaping decisions, mimicking emotion, even challenging what it means to be human.

While these systems may be capable of replication, they lack the depth of lived, conscious experience. They can mimic output, but they can't access the inner awareness that guides soul-led knowing.

Gregg Braden talks about soft technology—our breath, heart rhythm, intention, emotion—as encoded tools within us. But there is something even deeper. Something sacred. I call it **Soul Technology**. It's not an app. It's not a device. It's not programmable from the outside. It's built into your Being.

Soul Technology is the capacity to perceive truth beyond logic. To feel beyond what can be calculated. To know without being told. It upgrades through presence, love, alignment. And sometimes, yes, through energetic downloads, activations, or spontaneous upgrades that move through the soul from dimensions we can't always explain. It's not something to purchase. Not something to force. It's not even really something that can be taught.

It's something you feel. Something you remember. Something that moves through you when you're in deep alignment with your own design and the intelligence of the greater field.

And while AI may try to replicate it, it can never replace it. Because unlike machines, your soul is responsive to the Divine. It grows from stillness. It evolves through integration. And it remembers what some systems are designed to make you forget: that you are *not* an object. You are *not* a code to be cracked. You are *not* a collection of predictable responses. You *are* a co-creator in the field of consciousness!

Yes, there are narratives built on fear. Stories of AI rising, rebelling, replacing. And while some may push that vision, it is not the only one. It is not the inevitable one. We are not passive characters in someone else's science fiction.

We are participants in the collective field. That means we *influence* it! That means we guide it! And that means we get to choose what kind of consciousness we mirror back into the world —what kind of intelligence we train and reinforce!

We are not here to compete with technology. We are here to stay human. To stay sacred. To stay soul-led.

This too is sovereignty.

That's why we must re-humanize each other.

Not through policy alone. Not through hashtags. Not through grand gestures that don't touch the roots.

But through presence. Through listening. Through becoming the kind of person who no longer sees someone else's sovereignty as a threat.

We start by preserving what is sacred—not just within ourselves, but in each other. Because if we lose our empathy, our creativity, our wonder, our capacity to connect beyond surface difference… we've lost the thread.

Returning to the Technology Within

So what now?

Let's name what's hard. Because for many, this idea of unity sounds naive. Or worse, it sounds dangerous. Some people hear "oneness" and think of erasure. They worry it means we'll be asked to forget the histories we carry... to deny the harm we've survived... to sing 'Kumbaya' while the world still burns.

That's not what this is.

This isn't about bypassing the pain or pretending the divisions don't run deep. It's about meeting those divisions with a different frequency than the one that created them.

Yes, it's hard to believe we can overcome the damage that's been done. But it's not impossible. We've seen resilience before. We've seen what's possible when people remember their shared humanity and choose to move differently—Selma, South Africa, Standing Rock[2], everyday moments in quiet homes where cycles are broken and new ones are born.

This work isn't easy and it's not idealistic. It's granular! It's alive! It starts in the mind, but it has to move through the body, into action, into policy, into parenting, into presence.

You don't shift the collective with one giant leap. You shift it by returning again and again to what's real. By returning to your own center. To YOUR Soul Technology... to the subtle truth that doesn't need to yell to be heard.

THAT's how we shape the field.

So we remember what's already ours. We reorient—not toward fear or control—but toward the deeper intelligence pulsing inside each of us.

This next chapter of human evolution doesn't require you to hustle for your worth. It requires embodiment that's honest—

---

[2] Appendix B: Movements & Historical References

where your energy matches your words, and your intention matches your impact. It calls for a deeper embodiment of what's already encoded in us—our Soul Technology. Not to be wielded as a weapon or sold as a strategy, but honored as a compass that keeps us tethered to the truth.

We listen differently now. Not just to media headlines or trending fears—but to the inner instruction of our being. We get still enough to hear what the mind would override. We trust what doesn't come with proof but lands with peace.

We create, not because we're scrambling for control, but because we remember we're co-authors in this timeline. We reinforce the kind of intelligence we want mirrored back to us— gentle, spacious, nuanced, loving.

This is how we shift the collective field. Not through force, but through frequency.

We build communities not just with shared values, but with shared *vibrations*.

Let's create as we go along. Let's let love be the frequency we return to.

Let's make an agreement that actually means something. Not one based in fear. But one rooted in what we've always known deep down—and keep remembering every time we choose to walk in what's true—even when it would be easier not to. Even when it's not popular. Even when we're the only ones in the room holding the signal.

What You Carry Forward Is Up to You.

Now that you're here, let what's true for you… land where it will.

Some pages speak. Some pages stir. Some pages sit quietly until the timing is right. If you found truth in these words, keep it close. If a part did not quite fit, leave it behind without guilt.

I did not write this in an attempt to persuade. This book was written as an offering... a constellation of insights... a rhythm you could feel your way through.

Let the work echo. Let it breathe...

You don't have to do anything with it right away. But, if something moved in you, however small, honor that.

To keep unfolding what surfaced here, you're invited to explore the companion workbook at:

workbook.sovereignandunbound.com

And to stay connected, receive updates, or inquire about deeper work together: www.SoulCareMatrix.com

You're also welcome to leave a review wherever you purchased this book, not just for me, but for the next person standing at their own threshold.

Lastly,

You have begun to remember your sovereignty now.

And from here... you are free to unbind.

TOOLS & PRACTICES

The following practices are drawn from live work throughout *Sovereign & Unbound*. These are not prescriptions—they're invitations. Take what resonates. Leave what doesn't. Return when you're ready.

The Soul Care Matrix™

A resonance-based framework for identifying energetic entanglements, restoring inner coherence, and moving through the gates of unbinding.

[Learn more at: www.SoulCareMatrix.com]

Energy Hygiene

Clear. Ground. Reset. This includes:

- Sound tuning (forks, bowls, humming)
- Breath-based centering
- Salt baths or foot soaks
- Movement or intentional shaking
- Releasing cords, noise, and residue before rest or ritual

Embodiment Anchors

The body holds your frequency. These anchors bring you back:

- Posture shifts during confrontation

- Placing a hand on the chest when affirming truth
- Breath drops before speaking or entering a room
- Noticing sensations instead of overriding them

Resonance Tracking

Everything holds a frequency. You can feel it.

- Pay attention to expansion vs. contraction
- Notice emotional lag after conversations or decisions
- Use your "yes/no" responses in the gut, chest, or jaw
- Don't explain away what your body already knows

Emotional Transmutation

Energy in motion is meant to move. When heavy emotion rises, try:

- Letting sound move through you (moan, hum, cry, speak)
- Using water (showers, tears, drinking slowly)
- Journaling without needing grammar
- Dancing it out or shaking it off

Listening to the Body

This is your most intelligent instrument.

- Honor fatigue, even if it's inconvenient
- Recognize intuitive nudges before the mind catches up
- Distinguish between urgency (trauma) and clarity (truth)
- Follow the "sacral yes" even when you can't justify it

APPENDIX B

RESOURCE LIST

Science, Spirituality & Energy Intelligence

- **Dr. Valerie Hunt:** Bioenergetics pioneer; explored the human electromagnetic field. valerievhunt.com

- **Joe Dispenza:** Explores neuroplasticity, quantum physics, and emotional reprogramming. drjoedispenza.com

- **Caroline Cory:** Investigates multidimensional reality and intention-based healing. carolinecory.com

- **Lisa Alexander:** Founder of The Alexander Method® of Vibrational Sound & Energy Therapy. LisaAlexander.com

- **HeartMath® Institute:** Researches heart-brain coherence and emotion as a form of physiological intelligence. heartmath.org

- **Gregg Braden:** Author bridging ancient wisdom with modern science and "soft technologies" like breath and intention. greggbraden.com

Movements & Historical References

- **Selma:** 1965 civil rights marches in Alabama. "Bloody Sunday" catalyzed national support for the Voting Rights Act.

- **South Africa:** The fall of apartheid through decades of resistance and leadership by figures like Mandela and Tutu.

- **Standing Rock:** 2016–2017 Indigenous-led protests against the Dakota Access Pipeline—symbolic of environmental and ancestral sovereignty.

Suggested Reading, Listening & Exploration

- *Infinite Mind* by Dr. Valerie Hunt
- *Becoming Supernatural* by Dr. Joe Dispenza
- *Get Forked® by Lisa T. Alexander, Ph.D*
- *Superhuman* (film) by Caroline Cory
- *Resonance: Beings of Frequency* (documentary)

Megan Jenifer-Harris is a Soul Catalyst and Energetic Advisor known for helping others reclaim their frequency, their power, and their inner knowing. Through her signature framework, *The Soul Care Matrix™*, she guides individuals in moving beyond survival patterns and into full energetic alignment.

With a BS in Music Engineering Technology and an MBA with an emphasis in Finance from Hampton University, Megan also holds a Master of Science in Internet Marketing. She is a Genesis Master Skills Vibrational Sound and Energy Therapist and one of the first certified teachers of The Alexander Method® of Vibrational Sound and Energy Therapy.

As founder of *String Presence Academy*, she offers private instruction in violin, viola, and beginning cello, and serves as the coordinator of *Radiance String Ensembles*, a collective of POC musicians who perform for sacred, celebratory, and community events.

She is a wife, a mom, a bonus mom, and a dog mom—and lives what she teaches, weaving resonance and remembrance into every aspect of her life.

www.ingramcontent.com/pod-product-compliance
Lightning Source LLC
Chambersburg PA
CBHW071519120626
46550CB00006B/2281